Monographs
of the
Society for
Asian and
Comparative
Philosophy,
no. 1

he Sage and Society: The Life and hought of Ho Hsin-yin

nald G. Dimberg

THE UNIVERSITY PRESS OF HAWAII

THE SAGE AND SOCIETY: THE LIFE AND THOUGHT OF

HO HSIN-YIN

The Society for Asian and Comparative Philosophy, organized in 1967, aims to serve the professional interests of scholars involved in Asian and Comparative Philosophy, to advance the development of these disciplines in the academic world, and to bring Asian and Western philosophers together for a mutual beneficial exchange of ideas. With a membership of over 200 scholars and advanced students, the Society holds annual meetings and sponsors panels and workshops on themes of both scholarly and topical interest.

The Society also sponsors a monograph series on specialized topics in Asian and Comparative philosophy. The monographs are more detailed than journal articles and more specialized and of shorter length than standard books. Editorial inquiries should be sent directly to the members of the Executive Committee of the Society, Kenneth K. Inada, President; Bimal K. Matilal, Vice-President; and Eliot Deutsch, Secretary-Treasurer.

THE SAGE AND SOCIETY: THE LIFE AND THOUGHT OF

HO HSIN-YIN

Ronald G. Dimberg

MONOGRAPH NO. 1 OF THE

SOCIETY FOR ASIAN AND COMPARATIVE PHILOSOPHY

THE UNIVERSITY PRESS OF HAWAII

1974

Library of Congress Catalog Card Number 74-11085

ISBN 0-8248-0347-7

For my Mother and Father

CONTENTS

LIST OF ABBREVIATIONS

HHYC   Jung Chao-tsu [容肇祖] (ed.). <u>Ho</u>
<u>Hsin-yin</u> <u>chi</u> [何心隱集].
Peking: Chung-hua shu-chü, 1960.

MJHA   Huang Tsung-hsi [黃宗羲]. <u>Ming-ju</u>
<u>hsüeh-an</u> [明儒學案]. 12
vols. Shanghai: Shang-wu yin-shu
kuan, 1930.

MSCSPM   Ku Ying-t'ai [谷應泰]. <u>Ming-shih</u>
<u>chi-shih</u> <u>pen-mo</u> [明史紀事
本末]. 2 vols., consecutive
pagination. Taipei: San-min shu-
chü, 1963.

AUTHOR'S ACKNOWLEDGMENTS

My deepest appreciation and gratitude goes to
Professor William Theodore de Bary who gave freely
of his time to offer guidance, answer questions and
make penetrating suggestions while this study was
in preparation. I am especially grateful for his
patience and encouragement. Suggestions offered
by Professor Chao-ying Fang proved invaluable in preparing the translation of portions of Ho Hsin-yin's
works. Professor Wing-tsit Chan generously offered
to read the manuscript and his criticism and
suggestions improved it greatly. I am also in-
debted to Professor Henry Rosement, Jr., for his
painstaking reading of the manuscript and for his
careful guidance in its final preparation. I have
tried to do justice to the suggestions and advice
offered by each of these scholars. For the
insufficiencies of this study, and the errors of
judgment and interpretation it contains, I alone
am responsible.

I also wish to acknowledge the help of Liu Yü-yün
my teacher while doing research for this study in
Taiwan under the auspices of a Fulbright-Hays
Fellowship. Mr. Richard T. Wang of the University
of Virginia deserves thanks for his assistance in

preparing the Glossary. I am also grateful to Mrs. Floris Sakamoto of the University of Hawaii for preparing the manuscript for publication. And I shall be forever grateful to my wife, Arletta, for her understanding and patience as I pursue the study of Chinese thought.

Ronald G. Dimberg

May, 1974

THE SAGE AND SOCIETY: THE TRADITIONAL VIEW

The purpose of this study of the life and thought of the sixteenth-century intellectual Ho Hsin-yin[a] is to analyze his approach to the threefold problem of the individual in relation to society, his ultimate potential as a human being, and how best to fulfill that potential. This is a problem that had occupied Chinese thinkers since early times, but it became particularly acute during the sixteenth century amidst the confusion and uncertainty created by rapid social and cultural change. One result of this was that long established attitudes and assumptions concerning the individual in society were reappraised by men like Ho Hsin-yin--men sensitive to the needs of the individual in a changing world.

Ho Hsin-yin was one of the most active thinkers and social reformers in mid-sixteenth century China. As a perceptive observer of Ming society and a social activist who pursued his goals with unrelenting passion, he touched many men's lives. He exemplifies the vitality of the period, a vitality that was responsible for changing social, political and philosophical attitudes. In his own particular case, his

changing attitudes, the new and at times unorthodox
concerns he expressed, give rise to the fundamental
question of what it meant to be a Confucian, the
amount of philosophical freedom an individual could
exercise while yet remaining a Confucian. Ho was
associated with the T'ai-chou School[b] of Neo-Confucianism, and he considered himself to be the de-
fender of the authentic but beleaguered Confucian
tradition. But his lifestyle and his writings inspired contemporaries and later historians of the
period to question his fidelity to the Confucian
tradition and to denounce him as having Taoist or
Chanist leanings. The validity of such criticism
will be discussed later. For the moment suffice
it to say that this study will show that while Ho
did alter the Confucian value system in a substantial
way to make Confucianism answer to the changing
needs of the individual, he stayed well within the
bounds of Confucian social and moral philosophy.

The Confucian approach to the problem of the individual[1] was signaled by Confucius in a remark to
one of his disciples who had just been told by a re-
cluse that, because of rising disorder in the realm,
he should "follow one who flees the whole world."[2]
Specifically repudiating the reclusive life as a
valid role for the individual, Confucius said that
"one cannot herd together with birds and beasts.

If I am not to be a man among other men, then
what am I to be? If the Way prevailed in the
world, I should not be trying to alter things."[3]
According to this statement, the individual
assumed significance as a human being for Confucius only in relation to other individuals. He
exists as a true man only as an integral part of
society. But simply to reside among men is not
enough; gregariousness is not the mark of the
true man. Rather, what distinguishes man from
lower forms of life is his innate moral conscience,
his inborn sense of obligation to make the Way of
Heaven prevail in the world. To do this, he must
manifest the Way of Heaven in his own life by showing an active concern for his fellowmen, and by
attempting to reduce the suffering and increase the
welfare of those around him. This is what Confucius
meant when he said that he was trying to change the
world. He sought self-fulfillment by making the
Way prevail among his fellowmen, in this way contributing to their spiritual development.

In a sense, the real significance of Confucius'
remark is that it focuses attention on Confucianism
as a doctrine of human and humane action.[4] Confucius was not interested in the Way of Heaven as an
abstract concept, but in its practical application
in the realm of human endeavor. Similarly, in The

<u>Analects</u> he discussed the practice of humanity
(<u>jen</u>^c)--the essential quality of man--and not its
abstract meaning.[5] Remaining true to the spirit of
The <u>Analects</u>, the Confucians stressed the individual's role as an active and creative force in the
world. Reading from the specific to the general,
this makes society the sum total of all men's actions and the inevitable interactions between multi-
tudes of individuals. To insure the welfare of
society and its members, the Confucians conceived a
plan of social organization wherein each individual
was expected to perform a specific function determined by his position within some social institution, most often the family, community or state.[6]
In conformity with Confucius' statement that reciprocity should be the rule of life,[7] a person's
function or role in society was understood in terms
of what is expected of him by the group and other
individuals, and what he could expect in return.
Thus was formed the complex system of reciprocal
obligations and moral relations within which man
was expected to refine his inborn sense of concern
and commitment and to exert his energies on behalf
of mankind generally.

There can be no doubt that the care and concern
that led Confucius and his followers to perfect
themselves within the social enterprise was inclu-

sive of all human beings. Their love for other
people was universal. But this does not mean that
they expressed their affection in equal degree for
all people, nor that they treated all people alike.
They felt too strongly about the natural family relationships for that. Acknowledging the importance
of the natural bonds that exist between family members, the Confucians defined the reciprocal obligations and moral relations which form the basis of
self-perfection in terms of degree or distance of
personal relationship. In terms of humanity or jen
this means that it involves universal love embracing
all people and at the same time the particular virtues which accompany limited personal relationships
within the family, such as filial piety and brotherly submission. Thus could Confucius' disciple say
that "filial piety and brotherly submission are the
roots of humanity."[8] In terms of the individual's
moral obligation, this means that while he has a
responsibility to all mankind, his most immediate
responsibility is to the members of his own family.
To be able to fulfill these limited moral obligations without losing his identity as a true human
being--that is, to practice filial piety and fraternal submission without losing sight of his broader commitment to all the world--was the mark of
the Confucian sage.

In response to the demands of sagehood--the dual stress on the universality and particularity of humanity--there evolved within the Confucian tradition a process of self-cultivation with two complementary aspects: moral discipline or self-restraint and spiritual enlargement. Moral discipline is achieved by adhering to the ritual rules of conduct governing one's position within one or another social institution; and spiritual enlargement is the result of studying and mastering the literature and civil and civilizing arts of established culture. This is what Confucius' disciple meant when he said that "the Master. . . broadens me with culture and restrains me with ritual."[9]

The result of this process of self-cultivation is the chün-tzu[d], the Confucian noble-man who has attained the highest moral and intellectual achievements.[10] His refined sense of care and concern naturally led him into public service to look after the spiritual and material welfare of the masses through the established apparatus of government. Ideally, the sage should be the king whose exemplary behavior serves as a standard of conduct for the people. But because not all kings are sages and because not every man can be ruler, the model Confucian became a scholar-official, advising his sovereign and carrying out the imperial will. According to The Analects: "Not to take office is not righteous. . . . The noble-man (chün-tzu) takes office, and performs the righteous duties belonging to it."[11]

Either as sovereign or official, the Confucian noble-man fulfills his commitment to society as a member of an elite group. Four classes of people were distinguished in Chinese society. Specifically, in descending order, they were the scholars, the farmers, the artisans, and the merchants.[12] In conformity with the Confucian view of society as a corporate body of responsible individuals, each performing a function vital to the good of the whole, class rank was determined by what was contributed to the welfare of the social organism. The scholars ranked first in the social hierarchy because by demonstrating that they had mastered and could adhere to an officially sanctioned body of knowledge they alone qualified to govern society. Ideally anyone, even the most humble peasant, could acquire the education prerequisite to personal refinement and to gaining entrance into the ruling class. This egalitarian spirit was best expressed by Confucius himself when he said that "in education there shall be no class distinctions."[13] But in fact this egalitarianism was belied and the elitist tendency of the scholar reinforced by the insistence else-

where in Confucian literature on learning of such
breadth and depth[14] as to place a premium on qualities of mind possessed by few and educational
opportunities not widely available. This had the
effect of virtually denying to all but a small
minority the opportunity to develop true Confucian
moral value and to gain access to positions of
real political consequence. Classical Confucian
literature contains a variety of passages justi-
fying rule by this elite group and vindicating the
propriety of the special rights and privileges enjoyed by its members. To quote the most cogent of
these passages: "Some labor with their minds and
some labor with their strength. Those who labor
with their minds govern others; those who labor with
their strength are governed by others. Those who
are governed by others support them; those who
govern others are supported by them."[15] In strict
accord with the tendency expressed here and elsewhere in the Classics to ascribe an elite status
to the scholar, Confucian virtue was historically
identified with government service and with the
official bureaucracy.

It was not always a simple task for the Confucian to preserve his moral integrity while serving
in public office, however. Unfavorable political

circumstances often made it difficult for the Confucian to maintain and actively promote his principles. If he found the demands of public service degrading he was justified in Confucian terms in retiring from office to preserve his integrity.[16] But properly speaking the Confucian did not prefer retirement to public service. While in retirement he was expected to prepare himself for better days when he could return to his official position by engaging in the literary and artistic pursuits emphasized in the Confucian Classics. At the same time he could remain active in his local community as a teacher and civic leader. While these activities may not have been as overtly political as those of the government official, for the man who had retired from the government on grounds of principle, they could have strong political overtones. For him to continue to make a conscious effort as a teacher and local leader to promote his principles--principles at variance with those in vogue at court--was to engage in a form of political activity or, more accurately, political dissent. The most important distinction to be drawn between the retired Confucian who retained his commitment to action--as by definition a Confucian must--and the Confucian serving in public office, is the

amount of influence each could reasonably hope to
exert. Even the most energetic teacher or civic
leader could not hope to be as visible and effective as the man in a position of real political
influence. Nor could he strengthen his position by
identifying himself as the spokesman for some organized interest group or segment of society standing in opposition to established authority because
this would bring charges of factionalism. At best
he could hope to exert moral influence on a limited
scale until he could in good conscience return
to the government from where his efforts could be
more widely effective.[17]

In summary, the following points stand out in
the classical Confucian view of the individual or
self. The individual can achieve fulfillment only
by participating in the social enterprise and by
making an active contribution to the welfare of
his fellowmen. The moral discipline and spiritual
enlargement essential to self-perfection within the
complex structure of human society can only be
achieved by adhering to the objective standards of
behavior provided by the ritual rules of conduct
and by mastering the literature and arts of established culture. Qualified by perfect education

and moral development the Confucian scholar is expected to fulfill his commitment to society as a government official, though he may retire to preserve his integrity while retaining his commitment to moral action and to government service.

The Neo-Confucian approach to the problem of the individual was essentially the approach of classical Confucianism. During its development prior to the Ming Dynasty, however, certain attitudes became prevalent within Neo-Confucianism which reflect the peculiar atmosphere of the times, an atmosphere created in part by the confrontation between Confucianism on the one hand and Taoism and Buddhism on the other. To understand Ming thought and the actions of Ming scholars generally and of Ho Hsin-yin in particular, such attitudes which involve the Neo-Confucian view of the self and sagehood should be noted here.

The Neo-Confucian ideal was to transcend the self and to achieve identity with all things by affirming one's humanity, in this way to overcome selfishness. This is the theme of the Western Inscription,[18] a brief essay written by Chang Tsai[e] (1021-1077), second in the traditional line of Neo-Confucian succession.[19] Chang Tsai taught the reality and intelligibility of the realm of everyday human endeavor in opposition to the Taoist and Bud-

dhist ideas of non-being and Emptiness, and attempted
to furnish a metaphysical basis for the essential
ethical values of the Confucian school. In a work
entitled For the Correction of Youthful Ignorance,[20]
Chang Tsai described the existence of a single pri-
mal substance--ch'i^f or material force--which forms
and unites all objects in the universe. The Western
Inscription is one section of that work, and it des-
cribes the ethical implications of its author's theory of the unity of things: that all mankind and
Heaven and Earth should be bound together by the
principle of universal and impartial love.

The most precise statement of this doctrine of
the unity of all things and of its relevance to the
question of sagehood was made by Ch'eng Hao^g (1032-
1085). A relative of Chang Tsai, Ch'eng Hao was the
elder of the two brothers who are credited with
starting Neo-Confucianism off in the direction of
its final and full development.[21] Ch'eng Hao said
that "the man of humanity (jen) regards Heaven and
Earth and all things as one body. To him there is
nothing that is not himself. Since he recognizes
all things as himself, can there be any limit to
his humanity?. . . Therefore, to be charitable and
to assist all things is the function of the sage."[22]
In other words, "humanity" is both a cosmic and
ethical force embracing all things; and sagehood

is the realization of this underlying unity of
things and the impartial extension of one's love
and active concern to all men.

Achievement of the enlightenment and impar-
tiality of the Neo-Confucian sage required self-
cultivation along typically Confucian lines: moral
discipline and objective study. In the Sung, however, special attention was paid to the latter.
The value ascribed to extensive learning and to the
mastery of the arts by the Neo-Confucians was tan-
tamount to positing a cultural criterion for sagehood. This was particularly true of Chu Hsi[h] who
was responsible for giving final form to the Neo-
Confucian School of Principle, and whose commentaries
on the Four Books became the official orthodoxy of
the realm after 1313.[23] As explained by him, to
realize the underlying unity of all creation, the
individual must follow the teaching of the Great
Learning and investigate the "things" of the world
to learn their principles.[24] With Chu Hsi, the
"things" to be studied included human affairs--
matters pertaining to the world of man, the problems
of his society, and how to solve them. Self-cultivation required a thorough knowledge of the Classics
and Histories containing the principles which should
govern the affairs of men and the attempt to ac-

tivate those principles in the world. Properly
carried out, this process demanded daily study of
the written word for the constant development of
one's moral nature.[25] However, the important thing
was not simply to read a vast number of books, but
to probe and examine the principles contained in the
texts one does read to gain an understanding of their
essential meaning.[26]

Ideally, the wisdom thus acquired should be
applied on behalf of the people through service in
government. But biographies of major Sung Neo-
Confucians reveal a marked reluctance to accept
government service. For example, for more than
twenty-five years after gaining the chin-shih degree Ch'eng Yi[i] declined repeated offers of high
official position. He finally agreed to a government appointment at the age of fifty-two when he
became an Imperial tutor.[27] Similarly, Chu Hsi
refused numerous official posts and served in the
government for only nine of the fifty-two years
that followed his acquisition of the chin-shih
degree.[28] Rather than take up the active political
life both men preferred to study, to teach and to
carry out literary pursuits. Regardless of the
reason--whether because of the Neo-Confucian scholarly and intellectual approach to the problems of

life or because of moral compunction on the part
of specific individuals--in terms of the Confucian
as both a scholar and an official, the balance
shifted away from the latter with the Sung Neo-
Confucians.

The tendency on the part of scholars to forego
involvement in the government was intensified during
the Ming Dynasty. From the earliest years of the
dynasty an increasingly large number of qualified
men were alienated from the imperial regime because of drastic measures taken by the rulers to
insure the loyalty and to check the power of scholar-
officials. The founder of the Ming, Ming T'ai-tsu [j],
was a man jealous of his imperial prerogatives, and
he could not permit the scholar-officials to function as a class in making policy or in resisting
his efforts to centralize authority in the throne.[29]
He made liberal use of court flogging, imprisonment, and the death penalty to discourage dissent,
and to repress the position of the officials as an
independent political force.[30]

This harsh treatment of scholar-officials
continued through the reigns of Ming T'ai-tsu's
successors.[31] As a result it became increasingly
difficult to find talented men to staff the government. Qualified scholars were reluctant to respond

to frequent proclamations calling them to court.
In the words of a provincial official who was destined to die for his criticism of state policy,
"in former times, those who were scholars considered
it an honor to be promoted [in office] and a disgrace to be demoted. Scholars of today consider
it to be their good fortune to be able to conceal
their traces and not be heard of."[32] According to
one student of the times, this was because "the
meshes of the net of the law were too fine; one
error on things under taboo, and it was difficult
to escape destruction. Accordingly they cast away
their opportunities for glory as though they were
battered shoes."[33]

But intrusion of despotic power into the lives
of scholar-officials was not the only factor making
government service repugnant to Ming scholars.
Equally as important was the effect that official
recruitment had on education and scholarship. Following tradition, the Ming imperial regime selected
men to staff government posts through a system of
civil service examinations. True to his suspicious
nature, T'ai-tsu kept a zealous watch on the con-
tents of the examinations to guard against slander
and the violation of literary taboos,[34] and to
insure the ideological purity of government func-
tionaries. He set the ideological standards for

by Confucian scholar-officials. Instead, commitment to egalitarian ideals gave way to jealousy of an elite status for some Confucians, and they resented having to work with people of lower social status whose education and moral development they considered to be wanting by Confucian standards.

So disenchantment with the Imperial regime and with government service on the part of Ming scholars can be attributed to a variety of causes; the application of despotic power in the realm of scholarship and in the lives of scholar-officials; the subservience of formal education to the state examinations; the commitment to uphold the orthodox-Neo-Confucian Ch'eng-Chu School; reaction against careerism on the part of under-educated men; and jealousy of an elite status. Regardless of why a man refused to serve in the government, in the face of mounting pressures to conform, his only alternative was to return home where he could support himself by tilling the soil and by teaching. And it was not uncommon during this period for the retired Confucian to forego even the active life of the teacher in favor of the solitude of his study, not only to engage in the literary and artistic pursuits stressed in the Classics, but to engage in quiet contemplation as well. This was done not so much to escape or avoid the problems of the world

as to reflect upon them, to deal with them as they
affected the scholar personally in his efforts to
preserve his life, to maintain his moral integrity,
and to remain true to fundamental Confucian principles.

The tendency among Confucian scholars to dis-
engage themselves from the active life of the public
official, and even the active life of the teacher,
continued throughout the Ming. But there was a
counter-tendency among some activist individuals.
The most notable example of this is Wang Yang-ming[o]
(1472-1529).[39] The core of Wang's philosophy is
the doctrine of innate knowledge (liang-chih[p])--
the instinctive knowledge of the good, the moral
intuition common to all men. In terms of sagehood, this devalues the intellectual and objective
knowledge stressed by Chu Hsi as a prerequisite to
self-fulfillment.[40] In Wang's view self-fulfillment
does not require the investigation of the principle
of things external to the mind; on the contrary,
one need only follow the promptings of his innate
knowledge and remain true to it in whatever he does.
Of special importance here are the closely related
ideas of the extension of innate knowledge (chih
liang-chih[q]) and the rectification of things, Wang's
interpretation of the term ko-wu[r], hitherto thought
of as "the investigation of things." A man is to

judge the character of things by his innate knowledge of good and bad as it operates through the
activity of his mind: his thought or will ($\underline{i}^s$).
As he engages in the practical affairs of life and
his thoughts are directed toward the various
"things" or "events" ($\underline{shih}^t$) that exist or occur
within his realm of experience, he is to accept what
is good and reject what is bad; or, in Wang's own
words, "rectify what is incorrect to return it to
its original correctness."[41]

Those of Wang Yang-ming's ideas discussed to
this point reveal an activist strain akin to that
in Classical Confucian literature. The extension
of innate knowledge and the rectification of things
involve action and the positive expression of one's
will to see goodness prevail among men. The true
value of innate knowledge is verified only by participating directly in the world. In its fullest
sense innate knowledge should have some practical
consequence as a guide to the participant's actions.
At the same time, for those actions to be valid as
a positive force for good, they must be based on
right knowledge. This is the sense of Wang Yang-
ming's concept of the unity of knowledge and action.
As expressed by Wang: "I have said that knowledge
is the direction for action, and action the effort
of knowledge, and that knowledge is the beginning

of action and action the completion of knowledge."[42]
Practically speaking, this means that the man who
comprehends filial piety and brotherly submission
is able to fulfill the obligations appropriate to
those virtues. On the other hand, only when he has
actually fulfilled those obligations will he understand what filial piety and brotherly submission
really mean.[43]

In a word, it can be said that the philosophy
of Wang Yang-ming is a philosophy of involvement.
Or as said elsewhere, it is "essentially one of
lived experience."[44] This is best exemplified by
Wang Yang-ming's own life story. In stark contrast
to other prominent Neo-Confucian scholars, Wang's
biography recalls the traditional view of the model
Confucian as both scholar and official. Between
1499 when he took the chin-shih degree and his death
thirty years later, Yang-ming spent nearly twenty-
five years in public office. As one of the most
active officials of either the Sung or Ming, he distinguished himself as an administrator, a statesman,
and a general.[45] At the same time, while on assign-
ment he was able to develop a mature system of philosophy. Throughout his official career he was regarded as teacher and intellectual master by an
increasingly large number of scholars in and out of
government, and his lectures and scholarly dis-

cussions attracted students from all over China.[46]

Even though Wang Yang-ming exemplifies the Confucian instinct for active political endeavor and the instinct of the Confucian scholar to become an official, his ideas of innate knowledge and self-expression opened the way for a movement that denied the superiority of the scholar-official class and claimed for the ordinary man the right of direct access to sagehood. Essentially speaking, this is the crux of what was taught by the T'ai-chou School, the so-called "Left Wing" of Wang Yang-ming's School of the Mind and the spiritual home of Ho Hsin-yin.

The T'ai-chou School is named after the native place in modern Kiangsu Province of Wang Ken,[47u] whose experiences and teaching provided the school with its ideological foundation. Ken was born the son of a salt merchant in an area with limited facilities for a good education and formal intellectual training. Because of the accidents of status and birth, he was unable to take full advantage of the facilities that did exist. He was forced by economic hardship to leave the village school at the age of eleven after only five years of formal instruction. Thereafter his learning was self-acquired. He had no aspirations of rising above his own status, and he never studied for the state examinations.

Nonetheless Ken had a deep sense of responsibility to serve mankind. It is significant that in spite of his lowly status and lack of formal education he set out to fulfill that responsibility as a teacher. He could do this because in his approach to learning he devalued the special intelligence of the scholar and emphasized the ordinary intelligence common to all—a person's innate moral sense. This is why he could celebrate the joy of learning as he did when he wrote: "To enjoy is to learn, to learn, to enjoy! Oh! Among the joys of this world what compares to learning! What learning in the world compares to this joy!"[48] He could write these lines because the learning in which he took so much delight is not the disciplined study of the scholar, but the spontaneous operation of innate knowledge in everyday life. Thus the joy of learning is not reserved for the man of special intelligence and requires no effort; for innate knowledge is "knowing without deliberation,"[49] and its joy is available to all, humble peasant as well as learned scholar.

In Wang's mind, when innate knowledge is allowed to function freely the heart is rid of selfish desires and returns to its original pure state. Wang Ken speaks of this state in terms of preserving the

self--the self naturally free of the partiality
that arises from material desires. He goes on to
say that those who are able to preserve the self are
able to love and respect the self and in turn to
establish a relationship of mutual love and respect
with other people.[50] And this, concludes Wang Ken,
is the "Way whereby all things become one body."[51]
Each person, regardless of status or intellectual
capacity, has it within himself to reach this state
of moral perfection and to be true to the Way. For
Wang Ken to be true to the Way meant to take an
active part in establishing it as the basis of moral
and political order. This was to be done by leading a dynamic and creative life in the world, revealing the way through one's actions. For some
this can be accomplished by serving the government.
But above all else, the sage is a teacher: "a
teacher to the ruler" and "a teacher to all generations."[52] So, said Wang Ken, if government service impedes the teaching of the Way, one should
follow in Confucius' footsteps as a common man
teaching among the common people.

For Wang Ken personally, to be a teacher meant
more than simply imparting a set of doctrines to
the people. His ideal was the "great man" who
traveled widely over the land working ceaselessly
to reduce the suffering of the people as a demon-

stration of his love for mankind. Wang Ken himself toured the countryside in a crudely made cart on which he had inscribed his vow to "travel to the mountains and forests in order to meet recluses and into the towns and villages in order to mix with the ignorant commoners."[53] But in spite of his deep-seated concern for the welfare of these people, and in spite of his strong egalitarian tendencies, there is no evidence to suggest that Ken ever formulated a program of social or economic reform. For him as for others before him within the Neo-Confucian tradition, the ideal was still the sum of all individual actions performed in the spirit of "forming one body with all things." This is because, in typically Confucian fashion, he understood social problems as problems of the individual man, not as problems of society generally. In one of his essays Ken says that those who do not measure up to the Way in their lives and therefore fall short of sagehood need "education in clear wisdom and self-preservation--that is all."[54] Earlier in the same essay "clear wisdom" is defined as innate knowledge, and "self-preservation" is discussed in terms of the free operation of innate knowledge in a person's life, ultimately giving rise to "the Way whereby all things become one body!" As a

teacher Wang Ken's objective was to awaken the
people to their innate knowledge and to explain the
Way as something that serves their practical needs,
not something obscure and out of reach of the humble
and illiterate. To enlighten each person to this
truth, to inspire each person to let the Way manifest itself in his everyday activity, was Ken's way
of solving the problems of society.

The T'ai-chou schoolmen, drawing on the example
of Wang Ken's life, reflected his vitality as they
spread his teaching through the land during the
sixteenth century. The school's designation as the
"left wing" of Wang Yang-ming's School of the Mind
is indicative of its composition and of its approach
to the problems of life. Symbolic of its success
in carrying out Ken's charge to reach the uneducated
masses, the T'ai-chou School alone could count among
its members so many men of low station. Commenting
on this phenomenon, Professor Ho Ping-ti said that
Wang Ken and his son

> carried the intellectual torch to the masses.
> Here and there in Kiangsu and Anhwei, where
> this radical wing flourished, we find
> agricultural tenants, firewood gatherers,
> potters, brick burners, stone masons and men
> from other humble walks of life attending
> public lectures and chanting Classics. . . .
> Never before and never afterward, in tra-
> ditional China, were so many people willing

to accept their fellow men for their intrinsic worth or did they approach more
closely the true Confucian ideal that "in
education there should be no class distinctions."[55]

As pointed out elsewhere, however, the T'ai-
chou School cannot be described as a movement in-
volving the lower classes alone. In spite of its
origins and the dedication of its founder to educate
the masses, members of the gentry class were significant in giving the school its over-all character.
It has been shown that of the twenty-five men included in Huang Tsung-hsi's discussion of the T'ai-
chou School, seventeen were connected with the
official bureaucracy and eleven had the chin-shih
degree.[56] So it can be said that within the T'ai-
chou School people from all levels of society were
brought together on the common ground of T'ai-chou
ideology.

But the influence exerted by the T'ai-chou
School at all levels of sixteenth-century society
and the convergence within its ranks of the high
and low cannot be attributed solely to the strength
of Wang Ken's teachings. Other factors were at
work creating at all levels of society an atmosphere
amenable to the spread of Wang Ken's ideas. Of particular importance were the continuing expansion of
the economy and progress in the techniques of print-

ing during the mid-Ming. An improved transpor-
tation system and the resultant increase in size
of the domestic market stimulated growth in agri-
culture, handicraft industries, and larger-scale
manufacturing. Further stimulus was added by the
development of China's foreign trade, particularly
in the sixteenth century. At the same time a more
widespread use of printing presses led to a wider
dissemination of knowledge and made learning more
available to people of humble circumstances. So
as economic production and commercial activity in-
creased and the general level of prosperity was
raised, more people from the lower segments of
society were able to pursue new interests in cultural activities normally reserved for the gentry.
Along with this growing interest in high culture,
an increasing number of people were entering the
official bureaucracy from the lower social strata.
This was especially true of people originally involved in trade and commerce. Among these people
"trade and studies thus alternated with each other"
according to one mid-sixteenth-century observer.[57]

Simultaneously with the penetration of high
culture to the lower levels of society, members
of the gentry class involved themselves in popular
culture. It was not uncommon for official families

to become patrons of the popular theater and to
amass large collections of popular fiction and
drama. In some cases the literati adopted literary
forms which evolved out of the storytelling common
to the streets and market places. And while merchant families frequently complemented their affluence with the high honors of officialdom, gentry
families who were unable to maintain their official
position had to go into business to survive.

So these were the circumstances prevailing in
sixteenth-century China: economic affluence, social
fluidity, and independence of established modes of
cultural and political activity confused normally
well-defined class roles and concepts. Functional
distinctions which traditionally reinforced a man's
security and insured his positive role and identity
in society were thrown into disarray by rapid social
and cultural change. As expressed by one sixteenth-
century writer: "In ancient times the four functional orders of commoners had their distinct functions, but in later times the status distinctions
between scholars, peasants, and merchants have
become blurred."[58]

These circumstances prepared the way for the
spread of Wang Ken's teachings throughout society.
He made Confucianism answer to the needs of all men

seeking self-identity and a positive role in the world amidst rapid social and cultural change. At a time of confusion and uncertainty, he taught that each man had it within himself to be the master of his own destiny. In terms of self-fulfillment, he identified within each individual the potential to fulfill the role of the Confucian sage: to make the Way live in the world. In this way he claimed the right of direct access to sagehood for even the most humble and illiterate peasant.

This is the legacy inherited by Ho Hsin-yin. But Confucianism is a personal way of life--something to be interpreted and applied by the individual according to the circumstances of his own life. The T'ai-chou School itself is marked by great diversity among its adherents on matters of political, moral, and ethical import. The purpose of this study is to show how Ho Hsin-yin applied T'ai-chou Confucianism to the problems of the individual and of society as he saw them, to determine his fidelity to the Confucian tradition as he tried to solve those problems, and to examine the capacity of Confucianism to answer to the needs of the Chinese during times of rapid change.

NOTES

1. The following discussion of the Confucian approach to the problem of the individual is based in part on Professor William Theodore de Bary's study in William Theodore de Bary, "Individualism and Humanitarianism in Late Ming Thought," Self and Society in Ming Thought, ed. William Theodore de Bary (New York, 1970), pp. 145-247 (hereinafter cited as "de Bary, 'Individualism and Humanitarianism'"). Any mistakes in judgment or interpretation are my own.

2. The Analects, XVIII.vi. Quoting de Bary, Wing-tsit Chan, and Burton Watson (comps.), Sources of Chinese Tradition (New York and London, 1960), p. 24 (hereinafter cited as "de Bary, et al. [comps], Sources").

3. The Analects, XVIII.vi. Quoting de Bary, et al. (comps), Sources, p. 24.

4. On Confucianism as a philosophy of action, see de Bary, "Individualism and Humanitarianism," and Hwa Yol Jung, "Jen: An Existential and Phenomenological Problem of Intersubjectivity," Philosophy East and West, XVI, 3-4 (July-October, 1966), 169-187.

5. On Confucius' attitude toward jen, see Chan, "The Evolution of the Confucian concept of Jen," Philosophy East and West, IV, 4 (January, 1955), 302-303. See also Herbert Fingarette, Confucius: The Secular as Sacred (New York, 1972).

6. The Analects, XII.xi; Mencius, IIIA.iv.6; Hsün-tzu, "Wang chih-p'ien."

7. The Analects, XV.xxiii.

8. The Analects, I.ii.

9. The Analects, IX.x. See also VI.xxv.

10. In this essay the term chün-tzu is rendered "noble-man" when the stress is on moral commitment and as "gentleman" when the stress is on elite status within society.

11. The Analects, XVIII.vii.5. Adapted from James Legge (trans.), Confucian Analects, I in The Chinese Classics (Oxford, 1895; 2d ed. rev.; 7 vols.), 335-336 (hereinafter cited as "Legge [trans.] Analects").

12. These classifications appear in the Kuan-tzu^V and are probably those of Kuan Chung^W, Prime Minister of the state of Ch'i during the seventh century B. C. and whose text the Kuan-tzu purports to be. Regardless of their origin, however, the classifications gained general currency among the Chinese. See T'an Po-fu and Wen Kung-wen (trans.), Economic Dialogues in Ancient China: Selections from the Kuan-tzu (Carbondale, Ill., 1954), pp. 51-52.

13. The Analects, XV.xxxviii.

14. The Analects, XIX.vi.

15. Mencius, IIIA.iv.6. See also Mencius, IIIA.iii.14; and Hsün-tzu, "Wang chih-p'ien."

16. The Analects, XIV.xxxix, XVIII.viii; Mencius, IIA.ii.22.

17. For a thorough discussion of the question of retirement from public office by Confucians, see Frederick W. Mote, "Confucian Eremitism in the Yüan Period," in Arthur F. Wright, ed., The Confucian Persuasion (Stanford, 1960), pp. 202-240.

18. Translated in de Bary, et al. (comps.), Sources, pp. 524-525.

19. On Chang Tsai's ideas and for a selected translation of his works, see de Bary, et al. (comps.), Sources, pp. 520-525. For biographical

details see the Sung-shih , Erh-shih-wu-shih
(Hong Kong, 1959; 9 vols., consecutive pagination),
VII, 427/1098; J. P. Bruce, Chu Hsi and His Masters
(London, 1923), pp. 50-52; and Chan (trans.),
Reflections on Things at Hand (New York and London,
1967), pp. xxxi-xxxii (hereinafter cited as "Chan
[trans.], Reflections").

20. Translated in part in de Bary, et al.
(comps.), Sources, pp. 521-524.

21. On Ch'eng Hao's ideas and for selected
translation of his works, see de Bary, et al.
(comps.), Sources, pp. 558-564. For biographical
details see the Sung-shih, VII, 427/1097; Bruce,
Chu Hsi and His Masters, pp. 41-45. On Ch'eng Hao
and his younger brother Ch'eng Yi, see A. C. Graham,
Two Chinese Philosophers, Ch'eng Ming-tao and Ch'eng
Yi-ch'uan (London, 1958).

22. Chan (trans.), Reflections, p. 19. For
a full discussion of the concept of humanity and
the oneness of things, see Shimada Kenji "Chūgoku
kinsei no shukan yuishin ron ni tsuite," Tōhōgakuhō , XXVIII (1958), 1-80.

23. On Chu Hsi and his ideas, see de Bary et
al. (comps.), Sources, pp. 534-557; Sung-shih, VII,
429/1101-03; Bruce, Chu Hsi and His Masters; and
Chan (trans.), Reflections.

24. de Bary, et al. (comps.), Sources, p. 534.

25. Chan (trans.), Reflections, p. 68.

26. Chan (trans.), Reflections, pp. 101-102.

27. Chan (trans.), Reflections, p. xxx.

28. Chan (trans.), Reflections, p. xxxvii.

29. On Ming centralization see John K. Fairbank and Edwin O. Reischauer (eds.), East Asia:
The Great Tradition (Boston, 1958), pp. 298-299,
313-317; and Charles O. Hucker, The Traditional

State in Ming Times (Tucson, 1961).

30. On the institution of court flogging see the Ming-shih (Taipei, 1962; 6 vols., consecutive pagination), II, 95/993. For specific examples of T'ai-tsu's use of imprisonment and the death penalty against scholars and officials, see Ku Chieh-kang, "A Study of Literary Persecution During the Ming," trans. L. C. Goodrich, Harvard Journal of Asiatic Studies, III (1938), 254-311 (hereinafter cited as "Ku, 'Literary Persecution'").

31. See Ku, "Literary Persecution," pp. 289, 297, 308, 309.

32. Adapted from Robert Crawford, The Life and Thought of Chang Chü-cheng, 1525-1582 (unpublished Ph.D. dissertation, University of Washington, 1961), p. 12 (hereinafter cited as "Crawford, 'Chang Chü-cheng'"). The official was Yeh Po-chü[x] who was executed in 1376.

33. Ku, "Literary Persecution," pp. 256-257.

34. For examples of distress suffered because of errors committed in handling examinations, see Ku, "Literary Persecution," pp. 274-293.

35. Jung Chao-tsu, Ming-tai ssŭ-hsiang shih (Shanghai, 1941), pp. 335-336. Adapted from Crawford, Chang Chü-cheng, p. 11.

36. See Jung, Ming-tai ssŭ-hsiang shih, p. 2.

37. Ku Ying-t'ai, Ming-shih chi-shih pen-mo (Taipei, 1963; 2 vols., consecutive pagination), I, 14/142-143 (hereinafter cited as "Ku, MSCSPM").

38. Ku, MSCSPM, I, 14/147.

39. Wang Shou-jen T. Po-an; H. Yang-ming[y].

40. This does not mean that Wang abandoned intellectual inquiry altogether. Men could still study the Classics, but sagehood was not contingent upon it. See Chan (trans.), Instructions for Prac-

36

tical _Living_ (New York and London, 1963), pp. 32-33
(hereinafter cited as "Chan (trans.), _Instructions_").

41. Quoting Chan (trans.), _Instructions_,
p. 279.

42. Quoting Chan (trans.), _Instructions_, p. 11.

43. Chan (trans.), _Instructions_, p. 10.

44. Wang Tch'ang-tche, _La Philosophie Morale de
Wang Yang-ming_ (Shanghai, 1936), p. 11. See also
Hwa Yol Jung, "Wang Yang-ming and Existential Phe-
nomenology," _International Philosophical Quarterly_,
V (December, 1965), 612-636.

45. Wang's participation in military activities
was at variance with the Confucian bias against
military affairs. See _The Analects_, XV.i; _Mencius_,
VIIB.iv; and _Hsün-tzu_, "I ping p'ien."

46. For the details of Wang Yang-ming's life,
see the _Ming-shih_ III, 195/2273-77; and Huang Tsung-
hsi , _Ming-ju hsüeh-an_ (Shanghai, 1930; 12 vols.),
II, 10/54-57 (hereinafter cited as "Huang, _MJHA_").

47. Wang Ken T̲. Ju-chih; H̲. Hsin-chai^Z;
dates: 1483 /?/-1540.

48. Wang Ken [Ming-ju], _Wang Hsin-chai_ hsien-
sheng i-chi (Peking /?/, 1911), 2/9b-10; quoting
de Bary, "Individualism and Humanitarianism," pp.
167-168.

49. Wang, _Wang Hsin-chai hsien-sheng i-chi_,
1/12b; quoting de Bary, "Individualism and Humanitarianism," p. 166.

50. Wang, _Wang Hsin-chai hsien-sheng i-chi_,
1/12b-13a; quoted in de Bary, "Individualism and
Humanitarianism," p. 164.

51. Wang, _Wang Hsin-chai hsien-sheng i-chi_,
1/12b; quoting de Bary, "Individualism and Humanitarianism," p. 164.

52. Wang, _Wang Hsin-chai hsien-sheng i-chi_,
1/7ab; quoting de Bary, "Individualism and Humani-

tarianism," p. 167.

53. Wang, Wang Hsin-chai hsien-sheng i-chi, 1/2b; quoting de Bary, "Individualism and Humanitarianism," p. 174.

54. Wang, Wang Hsin-chai hsien-sheng i-chi, 1/13a; quoting de Bary, "Individualism and Humanitarianism," p. 165.

55. Ho Ping-ti, Ladder of Success in Imperial China (New York and London, 1962), p. 199 (hereinafter cited as "Ho, Ladder"). Cited in de Bary, "Individualism and Humanitarianism," p. 171.

56. de Bary, "Individualism and Humanitarianism," p. 173.

57. Ho, Ladder, p. 73. Quoting Wang Tao-k'un. As cited in de Bary, "Individualism and Humanitarianism," p. 172.

58. Ho, Ladder, p. 73. Quoting Chen-ch'uan hsien-sheng chi, 13/2ab.

II

THE SAGE AND SOCIETY: THE LIFE OF HO HSIN-YIN

Ho Hsin-yin was born in the twelfth year of the reign of the Cheng-te emperor (1517) and died at the age of sixty-three sui in the seventh year of the reign of the Wan-li emperor (1579). He was known at birth by his original name of Liang Ju-yüan[1] aa, which he retained until 1561. At that time he became involved in political intrigue in Peking and was forced by considerations of personal safety to assume the alias of Ho Hsin-yin, by which he is now generally known.

Ho was a native of Yung-feng county, located in Chi-an perfecture, in south-central Kiangsi Province.[ab] By the time of his birth Ho's native region already had a long cultural heritage and a tradition of sending men to the capital to fill high bureaucratic posts. It has been shown that during the Yüan Dynasty (1271-1368) Kiangsi Province was one of China's most important centers of culture and education. It ranked first among all provinces in numbers of classicists and private academies, and was second only to Chekiang in numbers of historians, philosophers, and men of letters.[2] During the early

Ming Dynasty the province continued to be the academic and intellectual center of the nation. By the
mid-fifteenth century it had produced more holders
of the chin-shih degree than any other province.[3]
Even though Kiangsi was surpassed by Chekiang and
Kiangsu Provinces as centers of intellectual and
cultural activity during the sixteenth century, it
continued to be one of the most culturally and aca-
demically privileged areas in Ming China.[4] Within
Kiangsi superior facilities for education and examination were concentrated in the provincial capital
area of Nan-ch'ang prefecture, and in Ho Hsin-yin's
native region of Chi-an prefecture. Of these two
areas, Chi-an provided more chin-shih degree holders
than any other prefecture during the Ming,[5] and
stands second only to the metropolitan prefecture
of Shun-t'ien during the Ch'ing Dynasty (1644-1911)
for the highest total in any single dynastic period.[6]

Thus Ho Hsin-yin was raised in an area renowned
for its cultural tradition and the academic success
of its native sons. Because of the almost total
lack of information, however, it is impossible to
make a conclusive statement about what role if any
Ho's family played in the cultural and intellectual
life of the region. There are allusions to its
wealth,[7] and to the size of the Liang clan,[8] but

nothing is said about any of Ho's relatives gaining
prominence as scholars or public officials. But
regardless of his family's academic and bureaucratic
background--or lack of it--the little information
that exists on Ho's youth shows that he took an
early interest in the Classics, and that as a young
man he aspired to an official career. He gained distinction in his hometown as a diligent and adept
student, and as one anxious and able to assist his
fellow students in their work.[9] In 1546 his reputation spread when at the age of thirty he placed
first in the prefectural examinations to take the
sheng-yüan degree.[10]

Ho Hsin-yin's newly won degree did not entitle
him to official employment, however. At best it
gained for him exemption from labor service and a
small measure of prestige as a member of the leading
group among commoners. Nonetheless, success in the
prefectural examinations was significant as the
first indispensable step toward higher academic degrees and a career in the official bureaucracy. But
what significance it had for Ho quickly diminished.
Soon after winning the sheng-yüan degree, he heard
the ideas of Wang Ken for the first time and there-
upon abandoned thoughts of an official career.[11]

Ho Hsin-yin studied the teachings of Wang Ken
under Yen Chün,[12ac] at that time one of the most ac-

tive and vigorous members of the T'ai-chou School. According to Huang Tsung-hsi, Yen Chün learned Wang Ken's ideas from Hsü Yüeh[13ad] who stressed Ken's doctrine of self-respect wherein the Way and the self are identified as one.[14] Yen Chün's ideas reflect this notion and the next step philosophically in Wang Ken's teachings: that to manifest the Way simply required following one's natural inclination. According to Huang Tsung-hsi, "Yen believed that one should simply follow wherever one's nature leads, trusting its spontaneity--this is what one calls the Way."[15]

Yen Chün's belief in naturalness and spontaneity is exemplified by his life of uninhibited self-assertion. His commitment was that of the Neo-Confucian sage: to form one body with all things. As expressed by Yen Chün: "All people are my brethren and all things in the universe are united with me."[16] When put into effect in his own actions, this became the basis for heroic devotion to friends and anyone suffering hardship. When his fellow student Chao Chen-chi[ae], a high court official, was exiled in disgrace to a distant outpost, Yen Chün went along to care for him.[17] When his teacher Hsü Yüeh died on the battlefield, Yen Chün went in search of his remains and buried them.[18] These actions prompted Huang Tsung-hsi to call Yen a "knight-errant" (yu-

hsia ,[19af] a man who selflessly goes to the aid of
others in distress.

Accounts of Ho Hsin-yin's activities over the
seven years following his first contact with Yen
Chün and the teaching of Wang Ken are sparse. However, what little is known reveals a free and independent spirit true to the tradition of the T'ai-
chou School. This was most blatantly expressed in
the disrespect with which Ho treated the elderly
scholars of Chi-an,[20] and more subtly by his visit
to the home of a Taoist physician named Juan Chung-
ho.[21ag] These acts reveal two important facets of
Ho's character which were to manifest themselves
repeatedly during his lifetime. First, his out-
burst against the scholars of Chi-an is typical of
his audacity in challenging anyone he considered to
be erroneous in their thinking or unjust in their
actions. In this case his target was the knowledge
of local scholars and there were no repercussions in
terms of his personal safety. But in the future his
bold expressions of conscience in word and deed
would place him at odds with men of power and authority and would jeopardize his security.

Though Ho's audacity and boldness would account
for the most dramatic episodes in his life, however,
this should not be allowed to divert attention from
the other important facet of his character becoming

apparent at this time: the inquisitiveness of the free thinker. This attribute is already visible in the fact that he was attracted to the teachings of Wang Ken and Yen Chün; but it becomes even more distinct with his trip in the autumn of 1549 to visit Juan Chun-ho. Juan lived in Ch'ing-chiang in central Kiangsi Province, and was known to Ho as a man in his nineties who had cured a serious fever epidemic in his hometown. Ho's visit to Ch'ing-chiang was motivated by his desire to learn the secrets of his longevity and medical powers. By his own admission his efforts on his first trip to Juan's home were fruitless;[22] but he was to return to Ch'ing-chiang in the future and was to spend time exchanging ideas with other men of reported Taoist and Buddhist leanings as well.

The first month of 1553 marks the beginning of the first recorded period of intensive activity by Ho Hsin-yin following his introduction to the ideas of Wang Ken. At that time,[23] taking his cue from the teaching in the Great Learning that a well-ordered family is the basis of world peace,[24] he launched in Yung-feng a thoroughgoing program of clan reform. He argued that because each household and local institution was concerned only with the welfare of its own members, parochialism and selfishness prevailed among the people. To combat this, he centralized all clan activities, concentrating most heavily on cultural and educational affairs and economic and social welfare. Henceforth, all activities within these areas would be carried out on a collective and egalitarian basis.

Ho Hsin-yin believed that one of the major causes of strife and corruption in society is the concept of private ownership of land passed down along family lines. Motivated by the desire to protect and increase family holdings, said Ho, people indulge in graft and deceit to avoid paying taxes and prey upon their weaker neighbors. To rectify this, he reminded his fellow clansmen that land and even life itself were theirs as gifts of a benevolent sovereign. Therefore, they should take joy in fulfilling their obligations to him and pay their taxes in kind and in labor as a show of gratitude. To help them do this, Ho initiated a plan whereby a leadership group consisting of 108 men would oversee the collection of taxes by the clansmen themselves, insuring that proper and equal amounts were collected according to the season. What was collected would then be given to the local official in payment of taxes of the clan as a whole, not of each individual household. It was hoped that this would enable each member of the clan to share the joy of repaying the sovereign and, more importantly, that

it would instill in them the feeling of belonging
to one united clan rather than to numerous local
households.[25]

The machinery Ho Hsin-yin established to oversee
matters of economy was patterned after that set up
to govern the clan's cultural and educational affairs.[26] Perhaps the most vital aspect of Ho's reform program was his plan to educate all clan off-
spring--and the offspring of anyone else who was in-
terested--at a centralized location away from their
families. He conceded the effectiveness of the
village schools in educating the people in the ways
of everyday life, but he said that they contributed
to the narrow outlook and feeling of selfishness
prevalent in society. Their major shortcoming was
their small size. Aside from the hubbub created by
crowded conditions in a small classroom, the limited
size placed restrictions on the number of people
with whom a student could become acquainted. In
addition, students were allowed to live at home.
This meant that they spent most of their time with
the members of their own immediate families who were
accustomed to doting on their offspring. As a consequence, feelings of affection rarely extended beyond the narrow boundaries of the family.[27]

It was for this reason that Ho established a
school in his ancestral temple and named it, appro-

priately, "The Collective Harmony Hall" (Chü-ho
ah
t'ang). Here the students were to reside, carrying
on a collective life, to be reared and educated under Ho's personal supervision. To govern the behavior of the students, he posited a set of strict
rules designed to give maximum protection from the
restrictive influence of families and relatives.
For the first ten years families were still expected
to provide their offspring with the necessities of
life, though with frugality as the rule. If the
school continued to exist and to function success-
fully after a decade, food and clothing would be
given to each student by the clan, and capping and
marriage ceremonies would be held under its supervision.[28]

Ho Hsin-yin served as overseer of this venture
in communal clan living for six years. Then in
1559, after running afoul of the local magistrate
over a special tax levied against the people, he was
arrested on charges growing out of the death of six
county officials at the hands of recalcitrant tax-
payers. He was sentenced to death, but before the
execution the sentence was commuted, and he was sent
on garrison duty to Kueichou. At this point a close
friend, Ch'eng Hsüeh-yen,[ai] who was serving as private secretary to the Viceroy of Chekiang Province,
persuaded his superior to intervene on Ho's behalf,

and his sentence was lifted.[29]   But by this time

his reform movement in Yung-feng had collapsed--or

had been suppressed--and there is no record that he

made further attempts to organize collective commu-

nities.

During 1560 and 1561 Ho Hsin-yin lived in Pe-

king where he engaged in activities that were to

have a profound effect on his ultimate course in

life.   At the same time they provide valuable in-

sight into Hsin-yin's character and into the vitali-

ty of the T'ai-chou School.   During his brief so-

journ in the capital Hsin-yin had the opportunity to

discuss Wang Ken's teachings with such men as Ch'eng

Hsüeh-po[30aj], Lo Ju-fang[31ak], Ch'ien T'ung-wen[32al], and

the brothers Keng Ting-hsiang[33am], and Keng Ting-

li.[34an]   Four of these five men were holders of the

chin-shih degree.   Ho Hsin-yin's close relationship

with them in Peking and the close friendships that

were to develop over the years to follow further

exemplify the force of T'ai-chou Confucianism in

cutting across social strata to bring men together.

A similar phenomenon is manifest in another of

Ho's activities in Peking.   During his stay in the

capital he opened a hui-kuan[ao], a guild hall or hos-

tel, where people gathered apparently to listen to

him lecture.[35]   During the Ming Dynasty it was cus-

tomary for provinces and larger prefectures to es-

tablish hui-kuan in the capital to accommodate native sons who were in Peking to take the metropolitan examinations, native officials staying in the
capital, and native merchants traveling from one
region to another. That is, hui-kuan were intended
for the exclusive use of natives of the sponsoring
locality.[36] When Ho opened his hui-kuan, however,
he attracted people from all walks of life and every
region, cutting across social, political and functional lines of distinction. And so effective was
his appeal that according to Huang Tsung-hsi, of
those who assembled to listen to Ho, "there were
none who did not follow him."[37]

Examples have already been seen of Ho Hsin-yin's
boldness in challenging what he considered to be
error or injustice on the part of others. This
facet of his character expressed itself again in
two incidents that occurred in the capital in 1560
and 1561, and the reverberations continued to be
felt by Ho Hsin-yin until the day of his death. The
first incident took place in 1560 when Ho met Chang
Chü-cheng[38ap] for the first time. Chang was to dominate the government during the early years of the
Wan-li reign (1573-1619), and by 1560 he was already
the Director of Studies of the National University.
During a brief but stormy confrontation Ho showed
his disdain for Chang's erudition by challenging his

understanding of the Great Learning. After Chang
Chü-cheng had stalked out in anger over this af-
front to his intelligence, Ho predicted that Chang
would eventually become the most powerful force in
the country, and that "one day he will kill me."[39]

Some of Ho's sympathizers say that this confrontation with Chang Chü-cheng was the first round in
a feud between the two men that culminated in Ho's
death nearly two decades later. The most immediate
threat to Ho's safety did not stem from this exchange with Chang, however, but from his involvement
in the plot to impeach the infamous Grand Secretary
Yen Sung[aq] the following year. This is the episode
that prompted the name change from Liang Ju-yüan
to Ho Hsin-yin. More importantly, it represents a
major turning point in Ho's life because it led directly to his departure from the capital and marked
the forced beginning of his wide-ranging travels as
a lecturer and teacher. In 1561 Ho is said to have
joined a Taoist magician in a plot to use trickery
and deceit to discredit Yen Sung in the eyes of the
ruler.[40] Yen's dismissal did not occur until the
fifth month of 1562, but he fell into disfavor from
this moment, a fact that did not go unnoticed by
his associates. So under threat of reprisal at the
hands of the powerful Yen Sung clique, Ho Hsin-yin
fled the capital for the southern regions of the

empire.[41]

For the next 18 years Ho lived the life of Wang Ken's "great man" ranging widely over the land seeing to the welfare of the people, teaching the Great Way "so that not one person fails to understand it."[42] Relying on the hospitality and patronage of friends and associates in official positions Ho traversed south-central China from coastal Fukien to the inner regions of Ssuch'uan and from the mouth of the Yangtze River to the extreme southwestern portion of Hukuang, lecturing and conducting public discussions in the independent academies. The lingering menace of Yen Sung's henchmen seems to have kept Ho on the move for several months during 1564 and 1565, seeking shelter with highly placed friends, most notably Keng Ting-hsiang and Ch'eng Hsüeh-po.[43] But after that danger subsided he was able to travel and lecture freely throughout the south-central portion of the Empire for twelve years. Between 1565 and 1576 he lectured in at least a half dozen cities ranging from Hang-chou near the coast of Chekiang to Ch'ung-ch'ing in the interior of Ssuch'uan. The records show that of all the places he visited during that period, he logged more time in Hsiao-kan in northeastern Hukuang than in any other place. As he crisscrossed China's mid-section he visited Hsiao-kan three times, spending a total of at least

five years there. While the bulk of Ho's time between 1565 and 1576 seems to have been spent either
in lecture halls or on the road, he took time out on
at least one occasion to help a friend conduct official business. He is credited with making a major
contribution to Ch'eng Hsüeh-po's successful paci-
fication campaign against rebels in Ch'ung-ch'ing
in 1567.[44]

The security and freedom of movement enjoyed by
Ho since 1565 came to an abrupt end in 1576. Starting in the seventh month of that year a series of
warrants was issued for his arrest on charges of
banditry, and for the next three years he was sub-
jected to constant harassment by authorities. Un-
daunted and defiant--and still willingly protected
by friends in and out of office--he continued to
move about the countryside, lecturing and stirring
up discussion in the academies. It was while under
pressure from troops sent out to arrest him in mid-
1577 that he traveled to his hometown to mourn the
death of his parents.[45] He continued to elude
government troops until early 1579 when he was
finally arrested in the Southern Metropolitan Area.
He was beaten to death in prison six months after
his arrest.

Available information makes it difficult to
offer definitive answers to the questions of motive

and responsibility in Ho's arrest and execution.
An easy explanation would be that his close associa-
tion with the academies led directly to his death.
By the late 1570's Chang Chü-cheng had become senior
Grand Secretary and all-powerful at court, and he
was outspoken in his dislike for the independent
academies and anyone who lectured in them. In 1577
Lo Ju-fang, one of Ho's friends from his days in the
capital, was dismissed from his official post by
Chang for conducting public discussion in an academy
near Peking.[46] Similar action was taken against at
least one of Lo's colleagues in the capital. Then
in the first month of 1579 Chang ordered the destruction of the independent academies and denounced the
gathering of groups for the "idle purpose" of conducting philosophical discussion.[47] In response,
Ho wrote what he considered to be his most important
work, On Study and Discussion (Yüan hsüeh yüan
chiang[ar]) in defense of such discussion as the time-
tested and only valid method of transmitting the
Way. His arrest came within two months, and he
died at the hands of his gaolers six months later.
Ho Hsin-yin himself interpreted this course of
events as fulfillment of the predication he had made
19 years earlier in Peking. It is reported that
with his last breath he called out to his gaolers:
"The one who kills me is Chang Chü-cheng!"[48]

In fairness to Chang Chü-cheng it should be
emphasized that evidence against him, particularly
in the matter of Ho's death, is circumstantial at
best. Chang had good reason to resent Ho: the two
men were at odds on several issues, and according to
one authoritative source Ho publicly attacked Chang's
behavior and abuse of power and called for his re-
moval.[49] This same source records that the order
for Ho's arrest originated with Chang.[50] But there
is no evidence to suggest a direct link between the
suppression of the academies in 1579 and Ho's arrest
in the same year. Nor is there any evidence to show
that Chang Chü-cheng was responsible for Ho's execution. To the contrary, the bulk of the evidence
indicates that local officials in Hukuang Province,
the area of Ho's greatest activity, were responsible
for both his arrest and execution. According to one
account of Ho's death the Governor of Hukuang knew
that Ho had offended Chang in 1560 and was aware of
Ho's more recent attacks on him, and disposed of
Ho to ingratiate himself with the Grand Secretary.[51]
According to another version of Ho's death the Governor ordered Ho's execution in retaliation against a
local political rival who was one of Ho's closest
friends and associates.[52] Yet another account claims
that Ho was the victim of subterfuge on the part of
Hukuang authorities who, before complying with orders

from the capital to arrest Ho on relatively minor charges, altered documents to make it appear that Ho belonged to a band of rebels, all of whom had already been sentenced to death.[53] In light of this last account, which suggests that personal dislike for Ho may have led to his execution, it should be pointed out that he had a reputation of a man who possessed a talent for stirring up the people. Thus local authorities, whose reputations and careers rested on their ability to maintain order, stood to lose the most with Ho active in their areas of jurisdiction, and to gain the most by silencing him permanently. In any case, existing evidence suggests that local Hukuang officials were more culpable than Chang Chü-cheng in the matter of Ho Hsin-yin's execution. Further, though it is likely that Ho initially attracted the attention of the authorities by conducting public discussions in the academies, it appears that the additional factors of personal antipathy and the desire to please Chang Chü-cheng tended to exacerbate his situation in Hukuang.

In summary, four distinct periods are discernible in Ho Hsin-yin's life. First, the period from his birth in 1517 to his success at the lowest level of the state examinations in 1546. The little information available on this period indicates that it was devoted to preparing for a career as a bureaucratic official. Second, the period extending from his first recorded contact with T'ai-chou Confucianism in 1546 to his exile in 1559. This was Ho's first period of development as a man of independent thought and action, exemplified by his experiment in cooperative clan living. Third, the period of his stay in Peking during 1560 and 1561 when he formed lasting friendships and made dangerous enemies. Finally, the period from 1562 to his death in 1579 marked by his wide-ranging travels as a teacher even while a fugitive during the last three years of his life.

The motivating force behind the independent course of action taken by Ho Hsin-yin after 1546 was his sense of mission to the world and his active concern for the welfare of others. In spite of this common thread running through the last two periods of Ho's life, however, special attention should be given to the contrasting methods used by Ho during each period to fulfill his sense of mission. Prior to his exile to Kueichou in 1559 his efforts to improve the human condition were confined to the area around his hometown and to members of his own clan; but after 1559 the scope of his efforts was unlimited. More importantly, during his days as a clan reformer his approach to the human predicament stressed regimentation and the arbitrary application of strict rules of behavior; after leaving Yung-feng he stressed freedom and spontaneity and unrestrained self-assertion. All of this makes one wonder what caused Ho Hsin-yin to change his tactics after 1559 and raises the further question of the consistency of Ho's idea of the ultimate human potential and how the individual is expected to achieve it. The answers to these questions must await an analysis of Ho Hsin-yin's view of the self, sagehood, and society.

NOTES

1. T. Chu-ch'ien ; H. Fu-shan[as].
2. Ho, Ladder, p. 230.
3. Ho, Ladder, p. 227.
4. Ho, Ladder, p. 231.
5. Ho, Ladder, p. 246.
6. Ho, Ladder, p. 248.
7. Li Chih, Fen Shu (Peking, 1961), p. 87. Ho Hsin-yin lun. This piece also appears in Jung Chao-tsu, (ed.), Ho Hsin-yin chi (Peking, 1960), Intro., pp. 10-12 (hereinafter cited as "Jung, [ed.], HHYC").
8. Jung (ed.), HHYC, Intro. p. 2.
9. Huang, MJHA, VI,32/63. T'ai-chou hsüeh-an.
10. Jung (ed.), HHYC, Intro., p. 1 and p. 120. Citing Tsou Yuan-piao, Liang Fu-shan chuan.
11. Jung (ed.), HHYC, p. 120. Citing Tsou, Liang Fu-shan chuan.
12. T. Shan-nung[at]; dates unknown.
13. T. Tzu-chih; H. Po-shih[au]; chin-shih 1532; dates unknown.
14. Huang, MJHA, VI, 32/81. Hsü Yüeh chuan.
15. Huang, MJHA, VI, 32/63. T'ai-chou hsüeh-an.
16. Huang, MJHA, VI, 32/63. T'ai-chou hsüeh-an. See Chang Tsai's Western Inscription as translated in de Bary, et al., (comps.), Sources, p. 524.
17. T. Meng-ching; H. Ta-chou[av]; chin-shih 1532; dates: 1508-1576. Huang, MJHA, VI, 32/63. T'ai-chou hsüeh-an.
18. Huang, MJHA, VI, 32/63. T'ai-chou hsüeh-an.
19. Huang, MJHA, VI, 32/63. T'ai-chou hsüeh-an.
20. Huang, MJHA, VI 32/63. T'ai-chou hsüeh-an.
21. Jung (ed.), HHYC, p. 100. Citing Ho Hsin-yin's letter to the Commander-in-chief of Kan-chou

prefecture (hereinafter cited as Kan-chou letter).
Juan Chung-ho's dates are unknown.

22. Jung (ed.), HHYC, p. 100. Citing Kan-chou letter.

23. Ho Hsin-yin dated the start of his efforts at clan reform in an essay entitled "Chü-ho shuai-yang yü-tsu li yü" (Jung [ed.], HHYC, p. 70). In addition to this document, two other essays contain the core of Ho's reform program: "Chü-ho shuai-chiao yü-tsu li-yü" (Jung [ed.], HHYC, pp. 68-69); and "Chü-ho lao-lao wen" (Jung [ed.], HHYC, p. 72).

24. Huang, MJHA, VI, 32/63. T'ai-chou hsüeh-an.

25. Jung (ed.), HHYC, pp. 70-72. Chü-ho shuai-yang. . . .

26. Jung (ed.), HHYC, p. 70. Chü-ho shuai-yang. . . .

27. Jung (ed.), HHYC, p. 68. Chü-ho shuai-yang. . . .

28. Jung (ed.), HHYC, pp. 68-69. Chü-ho shuai-yang. . . .

29. Huang, MJHA, VI, 32/63. T'ai-chou hsüeh-an.

30. T. Chin-yüeh H. Erh-p'u^{aw}; chin-shih 1559; dates unknown.

31. T. Wei-te; H. Chin-ch'i^{ax}; chin-shih 1553; dates: 1515-1588.

32. H. Huai-su^{ay}; chin-shih 1553; d. 1569.

33. T. Tsai-lun; H. T'ien-t'ai^{az}; chin-shih 1556; dates: 1524-1596.

34. T. Tzu-yung; H. Chu-kung^{ba}; dates: 1534-1584.

35. Huang, MJHA, VI, 32/63. T'ai-chou hsüeh-an; Shimada Kenji, Chūgoku ni okeru kindai shii no zasetsu (Tokyo, 1949), p. 135.

36. On hui-kuan during the Ming, see Ho, Ladder,

pp. 208-209.

37. Huang, MJHA, VI 32/63. Tai-chou hsüeh-an.

38. T. Shu-ta ; H. T'ai-yüeh^bb ; chin-shih 1547; dates: 1525-1582.

39. Jung (ed.), HHYC, p. 123. Citing Huang, Ming-ju hsüeh-an T'ai-chou hsüeh-an hsü.

40. Huang, MJHA, VI, 32/64. T'ai-chou hsüeh-an.

41. Huang, MJHA, VI, 32/64. T'ai-chou hsüeh-an.

42. Hou Wai-lu, et al., Chung-kuo ssu-hsiang t'ung-shih (Peking, 1963; 2nd ed.; 5 vols., IV in 2 pts.) IVB, 958 (hereinafter cited as "Hou, t'ung-shih").

43. Jung (ed.), HHYC, p. 77. Citing Ho Hsin-yin's letter to the Magistrate of Ch'i-men in the Southern Metropolitan Area (hereinafter cited as Ch'i-men letter).

44. Jung (ed.), HHYC, p. 78. Citing Ch'i-men letter.

45. Hou, t'ung-shih, IVB, 1008; Jung (ed.), HHYC, p. 91. Citing Ho Hsin-yin's letter to the official in charge of military defense for Ling-pei circuit.

46. Ming-shih, V, 283/3286.

47. Lung Wen-pin (comp.), Ming hui-yao (Peking, 1956), I, 26/417.

48. Huang, MJHA, VI, 32/64. T'ai-chou hsüeh-an.

49. Shen Te-fu, Yeh-huo-pien (Tao-kuang ed., 1827), 18/38a.

50. Shen, Yeh-huo-pien, 18/38a.

51. Li Chih, Fen shu (Peking, 1961), p. 93.

52. Jung (ed.), HHYC, p. 142. Citing Keng Ting-li, i-t'ien chi.

53. Shen, Yeh-huo-pien, 18/38a.

III

THE SAGE AND SOCIETY: THE THOUGHT OF HO HSIN-YIN

In his appraisal of human nature Ho Hsin-yin stressed the importance of the natural or physical self as the prime mover in man's behavior. The physical self--including the mind as a single substance--places the individual at the center of the material world and defines his relationship with other things in his environment. He becomes aware of the characteristics of each object and phenomenon in his realm of experience as it stimulates one or another of his sense organs and elicits the appropriate response. Ho classified all things and occurrences in the physical realm under the generic term shih^{bc}, "affairs" or "things" of the world, when he said that "all affairs take form for a person through his physical being when he experiences their properties through sight, hearing and thought."[1] Moreover, man can communicate to others his own impression of the objects and phenomena in his environment through his faculty of speech. He can translate into sound the properties of other things known to him because of his physical co-existence with them: "Having experienced through sight, hearing and thought the properties of affairs . . .

a person makes all affairs known through speech."[2]

So Ho Hsin-yin ascribed considerable value to
the physical side of human nature. It is by virtue
of his own existence in the world as a physical being
that man is aware of what goes on about him and is
able to register his reactions orally. But in the
passages cited above, the physical side of man is
defined solely in terms of his sense faculties and
physical powers, and man himself is depicted as a
relatively passive animal. Ho's idea of the sub-
stance of the physical self becomes more vivid, however, in his statement that "[sweet] taste, [beauti-
ful] color, [pleasant] sound, and comfort are natural
to man (hsing^{bd}). They govern his desires."[3] That
is, the essence of man's physical nature becomes
manifest in his material desires. The physical body
may expose man to external stimuli and make him
passively aware of them, but his reactions are determined by his desire for pleasure. As he becomes
cognizant of the properties of the objects in his
environment, he seeks out what is pleasant and re-
jects what is not. Moreover, contrary to what the
Neo-Confucian patriarch Chou Tun-i^{be} said, Ho argued
that desires cannot be eliminated. To want to be
without a desire is itself a desire; so, too, is

fondness of virtue.[4] In the mind of Ho Hsin-yin,
desire is a vital part of human nature, and to
eradicate it would be to suppress life itself. "The
mind cannot do without desires," said Ho.[5]

If Ho claimed that the mind cannot exist without
desires, however, he also admitted that it cannot
tolerate unrestricted desires. "When desires are
restricted, then the mind is preserved."[6] To Ho it
was neither the existence nor the type of desires
that mattered; he was only concerned with their excessive numbers. He cautioned that "whenever you
long for something and express your desire for it,
do so in accordance with the Mean. Then your desires will naturally be disinclined toward becoming
excessive in number. Is this not restricting your
desires?"[7] Citing Mencius, Ho described what it
means to restrict desires: "To love fish and to
love bear paws are desires. To forego fish and to
take bear paws is the restriction of desires. To
love life and to love righteousness are desires.
To forego life and hold to righteousness is the
restriction of desires."[8]

Rather than eliminating desires, then, it becomes a matter of choosing among them. At first
sight this seems to be a negative process of self-
denial. But Ho Hsin-yin made it clear that to him it
was an active and creative process of self-perfec-

tion. "One restricts his desires, thereby fulfilling what is natural to him (hsing). . . . He restricts his desires, thereby perfecting what is appointed to him by Heaven (ming^bf)."[9] In a similar vein, Ho said elsewhere that

> the idea that [the desires for pleasant] sound, [beautiful] color, [fragrant] aroma, [sweet] taste and comfort are governed[10] by the ears, eyes, nose, mouth and four limbs, and thereby govern [the behavior of] father and son, sovereign and minister, and host and guest, and the talented and sagely, and govern their expressions of humanity, righteousness, propriety, wisdom and their adherence to the Way of Heaven is equivalent to the idea that . . . the physical being, speech, sight, hearing and thought govern the expression of respect, accordance with what is right, clarity of judgement, perspicacity and sagacity, thereby to govern the expression of gravity, orderliness, wisdom, deliberation and sageliness-- the idea in the "Great Plan" which comprises what it says in the Ten Wings to the Book of Changes about fulfilling what is natural to man through the perfection of what is appointed by Heaven . . . ;[11] the idea used by Confucius to complete what was left incomplete in the Book of Changes and in the "Great Plan", the idea about what humanity (jen) relies on[12] for its expression, about humanity being expressed by what is natural to man through what is appointed by Heaven, and about expressing what is natural to man in such a way as to give

expression to humanity.[13]

Conversely:

> The idea that expressions of humanity,
> righteousness, propriety, wisdom and the
> Way of Heaven are governed[14] by father and
> son, sovereign and minister, host and guest,
> and the talented and sagely and thereby govern
> their ears, eyes, nose, mouth and four limbs,
> and govern [their desire for pleasant] sound,
> [beautiful] color, [fragrant] aroma, [sweet]
> taste and comfort is equivalent to the idea
> that . . . gravity, orderliness, wisdom,
> deliberation and sageliness govern respect,
> accordance with what is right, clarity of
> judgment, perspicacity and sagacity, thereby
> to govern the physical being--the idea in
> the "Great Plan" which comprises what it says
> in the Ten Wings to the Book of Changes about
> perfecting what is appointed by Heaven through
> the fulfillment of what is natural to man. . .;
> the idea used by Confucius to complete what was
> left incomplete in the Book of Changes and in
> the "Great Plan"; the idea about what humanity
> relies on[15] for its expression, about humanity
> being expressed by what is appointed by Heaven
> through what is natural to man, and about ex-
> pressing what is appointed by Heaven in such
> a way as to give expression to humanity.[16]

This means that the physical and moral selves do
not exist for Ho Hsin-yin as separate entities. They
take on significance for him only as interdependent
parts of human nature. The physical self--the human
body, its normal activities, sense appetites, and

emotional drives--becomes fully developed in its
fundamental role of giving expression to man's
Heavenly endowed moral qualities--his share of the
Way of Heaven. Similarly, the moral self reaches
perfection only when its specific attributes are
given life in the world of man through the physical
activity of the individual. (Thus respectfulness,
accordance with what is right, clarity of judgment,
perspicacity, and sagacity represent the undeveloped
moral side of man, and are insignificant until activated as gravity, orderliness, wisdom, deliberation, and sageliness.) Therefore, as the physical
self gives expression to the specific qualities of
the moral self, it determines and governs the direction and scope of their effectiveness. The moral
side of the individual will be apparent within his
entire realm of experience as it works a benign influence on his every activity and endows his behavior with perfect benevolence. This is particularly significant when the individual gives expression
to his material desires. His gregarious instinct[17]
places him at the center of human society, and unrestrained competition among men bent on satisfying
their desires wrecks social harmony.[18] But when
endowed with the qualities of the moral side of man's
nature, desire and the move to gratify it becomes the
most creative form of human expression. And because

the drive for gratification is also the most dynamic
and regular form of self-expression, it gives life
to the Way of Heaven at all levels of human society.

Therefore, to Ho Hsin-yin the physical and the
moral become significant as they become one and reveal the quality of humanity in the life of the individual. Humanity, said Ho, is the mark of the
true man: "If there is humanity, then there is
man."[19] Significantly, everyone has it within himself to be a true man. Humanity cannot and need not
be inculcated from without. Citing The Analects,
Ho said that "humanity is the responsibility of the
individual."[20] In another place he said that, when
questioned by his disciples on how to manifest humanity, Confucius told them to "govern your sight,
hearing, speech and activities according to your own
sense of propriety."[21] Therefore, he concluded,
"when a person's physical being expresses respect
and gravity and his thought is sagacious and sagely.
. . , and he speaks in accordance with what is right
and in an orderly manner, views things with clarity
of judgement and with wisdom, and listens with deliberation and with perspicacity . . . , isn't this
to act with propriety . . . , in this way to manifest humanity?"[22]

In other words, in the mind of Ho Hsin-yin to
achieve the interdependence of the physical and

moral sides of human nature and to manifest humanity,
one need only follow his own innate sense of what is
right and wrong in his relations with others. Because man is a social animal, as the sum of the moral qualities of the true man, humanity meant for Ho
Hsin-yin what it does in traditional Confucian literature: activity between men. More than this, humanity assumes the proportions of a dynamic and creative social force. This is what Ho meant when he
said: "If there is humanity, then there is man.
Men manifest it in their relations together as it is
manifest by the individual man himself."[23] Humanity
is the quality which brings order to society because
it enables men to get along in harmony. Humanity
means self-perfection and the perfection of others.
Hence, the true man is a man among men. Self-fulfillment cannot be achieved in isolation from others.
Because life is sustained by giving expression to
desire, including the desire for human companionship,
the full potential of human nature can only be realized within society.

It is with this in mind--that self-fulfillment
can only be achieved by participating in the social
enterprise--that one should consider Ho Hsin-yin's
concept of restricting desires. As shown above,
Ho said that to restrict one's desires, it is necessary to express them according to the Mean, there-

by preserving the mind. Elsewhere he said:

> When one is discriminating in the Mean
> and holds fast to it, he is sincere and
> his mind is not confused. When one is of
> singular purpose in the Mean and holds
> fast to it, he is sincere and single
> minded. There is the mind: when the
> mind serves as master, it is the Mind of
> the Mean (chung-hsin[bg]); when it is all
> pervading, it is the Moral Mind (tao-hsin[bh])
> . . . . The mind that pervades other minds
> and binds them together and thus, serving
> as master for one man, serves as master
> for countless millions of people, is the
> Moral Mind.[24]

Thus when Ho spoke of preserving the mind, he meant

the Moral Mind. He envisaged a common moral sense

shared by all men who adhere to the Mean and con-

form to the Way of Heaven. This is a creative state

wherein the Way prevails in the behavior of men and

comes to life through their actions in the every-

day world. But Ho detected in man the tendency to

give his mind over entirely to thoughts of the flesh.

This destroys the bond between the mind and the Way

of Heaven, and the Moral Mind gives way to the mind

of man. Consequently, men are separated from each

other and there is conflict: "To make the mind fol-

low man requires little effort and is easy. [But]

with his mind so preoccupied, when a man concerns

himself with this matter, he naturally will clash

with someone concerned with another matter. And
when he concerns himself with another matter, he
naturally will run counter to someone concerned
with this matter."[25]

This is why Ho Hsin-yin stressed the importance
of restricting one's desires. They do not work a
hardship on the moral development of the individual
because they are bad in themselves. For example,
Ho acknowledged that selfishness is a problem for
man, but as will be seen, he did not ascribe its
cause to material desire.[26] Rather, Ho said that
if allowed to dominate the behavior of an individual,
desires will subvert his relations with other people
and therefore preclude his self-perfection. Thus it
becomes a matter of adhering to the Mean and striking
a proper balance between moral considerations and
considerations of the flesh in relations with other
people. "What is natural to man is great," said Ho
Hsin-yin, "but should not be [too] extensive."[27]

But to give due expression to the moral side of
human nature is not an easy matter. In his discussion of the Moral Mind, Ho said that it is difficult
to conform to the Way of Heaven: "To make the mind
conform to the Way takes great effort and is difficult. It is as if the Way has been preserved, and
then as if it has been lost; one seems to possess
it and then seems to be without it."[28] In another

place, however, Ho stressed the natural affinity of human nature and the Way of Heaven: "The relationship between human nature and the Way of Heaven is as water flowing through the Yangtze River, the Yellow River, the Huai River and to the sea. . . . Water flows as a natural course through the Yangtze River, the Yellow River, the Huai River and to the sea; human nature as a matter of course achieves union with the Way of Heaven."[29]

This apparent contradiction is resolved in the light of Ho Hsin-yin's life and writings. A recurrent theme in his letters and essays is that the true man constantly exerts himself on behalf of other people. Each man has his own inborn share of the Way of Heaven, the essence of man; but to be relevant for the individual, it must become manifest in his concern for others. This is exemplified in Ho's own active concern for the spiritual and material welfare of other men which motivated him as a clan reformer in Yung-feng, as an opponent of excessive taxes, as a challenger of the unjust in Peking, and as a teacher and leader of men throughout the southern half of China. Ho had little use for the man who, feeling he has achieved all he can in society, goes into seclusion. To him, even though not in an official position, an individual should continue to work on behalf of the world. And

this, he conceded, is not easy: "When others speak
of retiring from public office, they speak in terms
of having achieved success [as an official]. But
when I speak of retiring from public office, I speak
in terms of continuing with diligence to put forth
effort. To retire after achieving success . . . is
easy. But to continue with diligence to put forth
effort is not easy."[30] Ho illustrated this by citing
Appendix II to the Book of Changes:

> Confucius was like a concealed dragon. Thus he
> said, "The element yang[bi] is concealed below in
> the earth."[31] The element yang represents fire.
> Fire easily flares up, but it is difficult to
> put it down below in the earth. If it is not
> put down below in the earth, however, it is not
> concealed. If something other than the element
> yang were to be used in this example, it would
> not be apropos of a dragon. For a dragon to be
> concealed is like the element yang being down
> below in the earth.[32]

Here Ho Hsin-yin used the example of Confucius,
who worked to reform society without being an official, as typical of the concealed dragon, symbolic
of the unemployed sage or noble-man. By claiming
that the dragon is analogous to the element yang,
and then identifying yang with fire, Ho proved to
his own satisfaction that it is as difficult for
someone out of office to change society as it is to
keep fire alive underground. Thus for a man to

retire to his home or into seclusion at the end
of his term of office or when he feels that he
can no longer fulfill the duties of that office in
good conscience is, in Ho's mind, to take the easy
way out. For his own part, Ho would emulate Confucius who "continued to exert effort with diligence
while out of public office with the feeling that he
had achieved success. Even though he was successful,
he continued to exert effort with diligence."[33]

Thus, driven by a sense of mission, the sage
labors indefatigably in the world in the manner of
Confucius and Ho Hsin-yin himself. As an itinerant
teacher unpopular with the authorities, Ho had to
contend with official persecution as well as with
the everyday problems of sustaining life. But he
continued to lecture and to hold public discussions
even as he was being hunted down just prior to his
arrest. Letters he wrote after he had been taken
into custody mirror his conviction that he was right
and that he could do naught but reveal the truth
through his own behavior.[34] He prized a man's spirit (i-ch'i[bj])--ideas and feelings--and lamented any
restraint placed on it.[35] Ideas and feelings are
common to all men, but they assume significance only
as they are exerted on behalf of others. This is
how a man achieves union with the Way of Heaven and
makes the Way live in the world. Said Ho:

The ideas of sages and worthies are always
sincere and, their ideas being sincere,
the sages and worthies always are sincere
in illustrating illustrious virtue in the
world. Being sincere in illustrating
illustrious virtue in the world, their ideas
are as one with the Way.[36] The feelings
of the sages and worthies are always nourished,
and being nourished, fill up all between
Heaven and Earth. Being nourished to fill
up all between Heaven and Earth, the feelings
become the mate of the Way.[37]

By illustrating the Way of Heaven in human
society, the sage contributes to the moral development of the world at large. But his commitment does
not stop there. Ho Hsin-yin adhered closely to the
view stressed by both Mencius and Hsün-tzu that welfare is the basis of popular morality; and to him
this meant that all men are duty bound to look after
each other's emotional and material needs.[38] This
is the basis for Ho's idea of nourishing the desires
of other people as the natural complement to restricting one's own desires. By choosing among his
own wants the individual merely reduces the chances
for confrontation with other men over the means of
satisfaction. But conflict is still a potential
hazard. To eliminate this entirely, each individual
must give active support to his fellow men in their
search for gratification. In an essay on the ad-

vantages of communal clan living, Ho said that once
the clan has been gathered together, "if an uncle
wants to lead [the clan], but has not had the opportunity, he will be permitted to act as leader for a
day and a night. Thus shall we gather together in
harmony, and nourish his desire to lead."[39] Moreover, when one has already achieved satisfaction,
he should share it with others: "Formerly, even
though Kung-liu was fond of wealth, he shared [the
power to satisfy] the same desires with all the
people. Consider the merit of the generosity of
former times and nourish the desires [of others]
accordingly."[40]

Therefore, the individual is significant for Ho
Hsin-yin only in relation to other individuals.
Standing alone, man serves no purpose: he cannot
achieve self-perfection himself, nor can he con-
tribute to the perfection of others. Life is sustained by the interdependence of all people in the
community. Ho learned this from his own experiences.
But he also believed that for self-fulfillment to
be achieved, the community of man must be free of
the restrictions imposed by vertical and horizontal
degrees of personal relationship. The essence of
man is the equal extension to all creatures of the
most intense feeling of love to the Chinese--the
affection reserved for father and son by the tra-

ditional system of family relations. According to

Ho's definition of humanity (jen):

> For the humane man there is nothing not
> kindred to him. He enlarges his feeling
> of kinship for a relative to all, and sees
> kinship not only in the relation of father
> and son but in all relations worthy of the
> feeling of kinship, to the extent that all
> who have blood and breath are considered
> his kin, beyond which the feeling of kinship
> can be enlarged no further. Such a feeling
> of kinship enables him to broaden his
> dwelling place to encompass the dwelling
> places of all-under-Heaven,[41] thus enabling
> him to manifest humanity.[42]

Similarly, Ho defined righteousness (i[bk]) as the ex-

tension to all beings of the feeling of respect tra-

ditionally due the ruler:

> For the righteous man there is nothing not
> respected by him. He extends his feelings
> of respect for a worthy to all, and sees
> respect not only in the relation of ruler
> and subject but in all relations worthy of
> the feeling of respect, to the extent that
> all who have blood and breath are respected
> by him, beyond which the feeling of respect
> can be extended no further. Such a feeling
> of respect enables him to straighten his path
> to reach the path followed by all-under-
> Heaven, thus enabling him to manifest
> righteousness.[43]

This interpretation of humanity and righteous-

ness explains why Ho turned from the nuclear family

to the clan and, when that failed, to the community
of his friends and colleagues for companionship.
He was always looking for the broader world, the
path followed by all-under-Heaven, so he could extend his love and respect equally to all men. If
to seek personal fulfillment in this manner made it
appear that Ho was taking a stance in opposition to
accepted forms of social relations, it was because
those forms were not in harmony with the Way of
Heaven.[44]

As seen earlier in this study, humanity and
righteousness traditionally have been defined in
terms of what is proper according to degrees of
personal relationships. The Analects say that "filial piety and fraternal submission are the roots of
humanity."[45] Mencius added that "the reality of humanity is this: to serve one's parents. The reality of righteousness is this: to obey one's elder
brother."[46] This attitude persisted through the
development of Neo-Confucianism, even though there
grew up with such men as Chang Tsai and the Ch'eng
brothers the doctrine that humanity would enable the
sage to "form one body with Heaven and Earth and all
things."[47] The traditional interpretations of humanity and righteousness continued to be upheld by
the Neo-Confucian School of the Mind. For example,

Wang Yang-ming said: "We Confucians accept the relationship between father and son and fulfill it
with the humanity it deserves. We accept the relationship between ruler and minister and fulfill it
with the righteousness it deserves."[48] But Ho Hsin-
yin's definition of humanity and righteousness is a
flat rejection of this interpretation and of what
he considered to be the attendant restrictions imposed on the spontaneous expression of the Way by
graded ranks of personal relationship. He had
judged the world and found it wanting in the qualities inspired by Heaven. The barriers of graded
love and respect are incompatible with the Way of
Heaven and prevent it from being expressed in man's
life. So, said Ho, feelings of exclusiveness and
selfishness prevail in the world over the ideals of
universal love and respect. The ruler belies his
proper role as the paragon of all that is good in
the world with his contempt for the ministers of
state; and the ministers in turn compromise their
own positions by toadying to the sovereign.[49] According to Ho's appraisal of the family as it existed in his day, the father-son relationship engen-
ders favoritism; relations between elder and younger
brothers are too partial; and husbands and wives
command too much attention from their spouses.[50]

In view of this appraisal of existing family re-

lationships, it is not surprising that Ho Hsin-yin
found in the family a major source of human hardship and strife. He complained that family elders
exhibit concern only for the education and material
well-being of their own offspring. Consequently,
the children know only the love of their parents and
siblings and express their own affection accordingly.[51] Furthermore, people consider that their persons and possessions are bequeathed to them along
family lines and thus fight to protect family wealth
and integrity.[52] Because of all of this a feeling
of privacy and even selfishness persists in each
household, and families become ingrown units. Finally, the selfishness works down to each individual
family member, whose "only wish is to have the entire household help him save on expenses and labor
while he himself ignores any need of the household."[53] In other words, the people of Ho's time
were void of the sense of social commitment that
leads men to nourish the wants of others and to
share with them the means of satisfying their needs.
On the contrary, because society was fragmented into
many isolated units, competition was rampant, and
the weak were easy prey for their more powerful
neighbors bent on self-aggrandizement.[54] This is
why Ho instituted his program of clan reform in 1553.

By exposing what he considered to be the faults

of Ming society, Ho set the stage for his own theory
of proper interpersonal relationships. In his mind
society is a continuum of the self, a collective
unit reflecting the qualities of its basic parts as
the sea takes on the quality of water.[55] According
to this notion the quality of social institutions is
rooted in human nature, and man's goodness or badness
is mirrored at all levels of human society. It
stands to reason, then, that man must first perfect
himself before his institutions can be rectified.
To explain this notion, Ho Hsin-yin elaborated upon
the concept set forth in the Great Learning that
"things have their root and their branches. Affairs
have their end and their beginning. To know what is
first and what is last will lead to the Way."[56] According to the Great Learning this means that:

> The ancients who wished to illustrate illus-
> trious virtue throughout the kingdom, first
> ordered well their own states. Wishing to
> order well their own states, they first re-
> gulated their families. Wishing to regulate
> their families, they first cultivated their
> persons. Wishing to cultivate their persons,
> they first rectified their hearts. Wishing
> to rectify their hearts, they first sought to
> be sincere in their thoughts. Wishing to be
> sincere in their thoughts, they first extended
> to the utmost their knowledge. Such exten-
> sion of knowledge lay in the investigation of

things. Things being investigated, their
knowledge becomes complete. Their knowledge
being complete, their thoughts were sincere.
Their thoughts being sincere, their hearts
were then rectified. Their hearts being
rectified, their persons were cultivated.
Their persons being cultivated, their
families were regulated. Their families
being regulated, their states were rightly
governed. Their states being rightly
governed, the whole world was made tranquil.[57]

So the perfection of the fundamental ingredient

of human nature, in this case knowledge, sets off a

chain reaction which ultimately leads to the paci-

fication of the realm. When Ho Hsin-yin described

this process, he used terms which underscore the im-

portance he attached to the problem of the relation-

ship between the individual and his social institu-

tions, particularly the family. He called the higher

forms of social organization chia[bl], rendered here as

"collective units," and said that they assume the

characteristics of lower forms, which he called

shen[bm], rendered here as "basic units." In Ho's own

words:

The mind, thoughts and knowledge are basic
units in the individual; the individual is
the basic unit in the family; the family
is the basic unit in the state; and the
state is the basic unit in the world. . . .
The world is a collective unit composed of
states; the state is a collective unit com-

posed of families; the family is a collective
unit composed of individuals; and the individual
is a collective unit composed of the mind,
thought and knowledge. . . . The collective
unit assumes the form and visible representation
of its basic unit.[58]

Ho Hsin-yin adhered to the notion expressed in
the Great Learning that knowledge is the root from
which all institutions grow. It is what man studies
and learns that determines the quality of his social
structure. This is because learning provides man
with a standard for judging himself and his institutions. It is important, therefore, that learning
be properly directed; otherwise man's standard for
measuring things will be untrue. Ho Hsin-yin revealed what he considered to be the proper focus
of man's study when he said:

> The standard for studying is not simply
> principle (li[bn]), but in fact is concrete
> affairs (shih[bo]). A scale, a marking line,
> and a carpenter's square are all alike [in
> that they measure things]. When in the
> unmanifest state[59] concrete affairs are
> concealed in principle, they are the
> equivalent of a scale which has not been
> hung up, a marking line which has not
> been strung out, and a carpenter's square
> which has not been set [to the wood]. When
> in the manifest state principles become
> apparent in concrete affairs, it is like
> the scale having been hung up, the marking
> line having been stretched out, and the

carpenter's square having been set [to the wood]. Whatever measures things is a standard; and whatever gives visible representation and form to its pattern is a thing (wu^{bp}).[60]

In other words, man should focus his attention on the practical affairs of everyday life because they represent principle in tangible form. In the mind of Ho Hsin-yin principle is the proper measure of all things. But to study it in its pure, latent state is not possible, for it does not fulfill its potential as the standard of what is right in the world until it becomes apparent to man in the practical affairs of life. Confucius knew this, claimed Ho, and thus studied men and their affairs, the common matters in the world, and for this reason was able to understand the lofty principle in them.[61] Men who follow Confucius in this are able to perfect their inborn sense of what is right and wrong according to the correct principle of things and use it as the standard for judging all forms of social organization. And only what conforms to this standard is to be counted among the true things in the world:

> A thing (wu) is principle and is a concrete affair (shih). A concrete affair and principle are things. Without things, there would be no standards. It is imperative that there be standards. When there are standards, there

are thus things, basic units and collective
units. A collective unit assumes the form
and visible representation of its basic
unit. A basic unit assumes the form and
visible representation of its thing. A
thing assumes the form and visible representation of its standard. It is imperative
that there be standards, but without things,
there would be none. Without standards there
would be neither things, nor basic units,
nor collective units.[62]

As might be expected, Ho Hsin-yin argued that
this was precisely the situation that prevailed
during his own times. This is what he meant when
he said:

Why are some people who today study Confucius'
learning deceived by the arts of immortality
and are thus unconsciously deceived by members
of the Taoist School? Without saying a word
they study, and consider that there is no
mystery unless one achieves immortality; how
can they avoid being deceived by members of
the Taoist School? Why are they deceived
by the spells of meditation and are thus
unconsciously deceived by members of the
Buddhist School? Without saying a word they
study, and consider that there is no Perfect
Doctrine[63] unless one practices meditation;
how can they avoid being deceived by members
of the Buddhist School? They therefore have allowed their basic units. . . [and] their
collective units to become confused with those
above and below, in front and in back, and to
the left and to the right, and without being

aware of it they have no [basic or] collective
units. What do they study that permits them
to end up without basic and collective units?
What are their standards? But even if they
themselves had abided by the teaching which
had not rejected the standard by which to
judge what is above and below, in front and
in back, to the left and to the right, they
still would have been deceived by members
of the Literati School,[64] and would still be
unaware that they are without basic and
collective units. The literati have been
unaware for a long time that they have neither
basic nor collective units. . . . They have
[also] allowed themselves to be deceived by
the arts of immortality . . . [and] by the
spells of meditation.[65]

When he said this, of course, he did not mean
that the institutions of the day were of Taoist and
Buddhist origin. He was simply lamenting the fact
that the framers of those institutions had been distracted by the mysteries of Taoism and Buddhism from
the proper study of practical affairs as stressed
by Confucius, and that the scholarly elite of his
own day had followed suit. As a result, they were
ignorant of the correct standard for judging forms
of social organization and for distinguishing the
proper from the improper. Hence, the social and
political institutions of Ming society did not measure up to the correct principle of things.

Ho Hsin-yin gave some idea of what it means for
a social structure to conform to the correct principle of things when he said that "birds and beasts
and barbarians all have blood and breath and Heaven
extends to all of them, bringing them all together
without discriminating among them."[66] In other
words, all things are equal under Heaven. Because
he knew the correct principle of things, said Ho,
Confucius practiced this in his relations with
others, discriminating against neither practitioners
of the arts of immortality nor the arts of meditation, nor against anyone "above him or below him, in
front of him or behind him, or to his left or to his
right."[67] Thus, "all sentient beings loved Confucius and showed their respect for him."[68] So as
applied to social organization, the correct principle
to follow is the principle of universal equality.
This is in accord with Ho's description of the true
man who comprehends the Way of Heaven and loves and
respects all people equally. In the mind of Ho Hsin-
yin, then, the ideal social structure reflects the
qualities of the true man and conforms to the principle of universal equality, allowing men to express spontaneously their love and respect without
regard for graded personal relationships.

For this reason the achievement of Ho Hsin-yin's
ideal meant radical social change. He saw all men

as members of a single family sharing a common moral sense and committed to each other's welfare. As seen in the story of his life, Ho was able to go beyond the limitations of the self, family, and officialdom and to find personal satisfaction only in the company of his friends. It is not surprising, therefore, that he stressed friendship as the one relationship between men reflecting the human ideal and encouraging fulfillment of the Way of Heaven. According to Ho, "friendship (yu^bq) is maintained by interaction, and the Way and its study is found fully in the interaction between friends."[69] But Ho's own personal commitment was to teach and conduct public philosophical discussion. This was his way of contributing to the welfare of the people of his time. Furthermore, the friends who offered him security were scholars and teachers and the everyday participants with him in his public lectures. So in his own experience friendship took on an added dimension and reached its ultimate form in the relationship between teacher and student. When he spoke of this relationship, Ho told more explicitly how the Way of Heaven is fulfilled in communications between men: "The teacher is not the Way; but the teacher does comprehend the Way fully. The teacher does not represent the learning process; but the teacher makes learning simple and concise. If the teacher neither comprehends fully the Way nor makes learning simple and concise, he cannot communicate with others. . . . The student (yu lit. 'friend') learns the Way from his teacher and thus is able to communicate with Heaven and Earth."[70]

A corollary of Ho Hsin-yin's faith in the effectiveness of the relationship between student and teacher is his belief that the process of learning and teaching carried on by them is ingrained in man's actual nature and is a spontaneous and irrepressible form of human behavior. As has been shown, Ho believed that man's awareness of everything that exists and occurs about him derives from his own physical existence. Therefore, he concluded, "study has its origin in the physical being."[71] Similarly, man's natural capacity to verbalize his own experiences and impressions gives rise to what Ho considered to be the only proper method of teaching--oral explanation or discussion of some issue or course of action: "discussion (chiang^br) has its origin in speech."[72] In the mind of Ho Hsin-yin, then, the ability to study and the ability to teach are undeniable companions in the natural makeup of every living human being: "when there is physical being, there is speech: so can there be study without discussion?"[73]

By identifying studying and teaching with the

physical self, Ho made them essential to the achievement to sagehood. As has been seen, the "Great Plan" process of self-perfection cited by Ho to illustrate the interdependence of the physical and moral selves starts with the actual physical nature of the individual and culminates in the fulfillment of the essential moral nature, with each physical faculty giving expression to an appropriate moral quality. To help make his point about the significance of studying and teaching, Ho summed this up as follows:

> Of the vital-affairs, the first, second, third and fourth achieve fulfillment in the fifth . . . . Physical being, speech, sight and hearing achieve fulfillment in thought. . . . Respect, accordance with what is right, clarity of judgement and perspicacity achieve fulfillment in sagacity. . . . Gravity, orderliness, wisdom, and deliberation achieve fulfillment in sagehood. . . . Sagehood brings sagacity and thought and all the five vital-affairs to fulfillment.[74]

What is important here is that sagehood is described as the sum of all of man's physical functions and moral qualities. Each function and each quality is essential to sagehood. The failure of one physical function to give expression to the appropriate moral attribute precludes the possibility of achieving sagehood. Conversely, sagehood represents the state of highest excellence for every component of human nature, physical and moral. And if this is

true of speech and hearing, it is all the more true
of the physical functions of studying and teaching.
As explained by Ho:

> Sagehood brings the physical being to fulfillment
> as it brings study to fulfillment. Doesn't
> the physical being give rise to sagehood as it
> gives rise to study? If a person did not exist
> as a physical being, he would not study and would
> not achieve sagehood. . . . Sagehood brings
> speech to fulfillment as it brings discussion to
> fulfillment. Doesn't speech give rise to sage-
> hood as it gives rise to discussions? If a
> person did not speak, he would not engage in
> discussion and would not achieve sagehood.[75]

And: "Exercise sagacity in thought, deliberation
and perspicacity in hearing, clarity of judgement
and wisdom in sight, and orderliness and accordance
with what is right in speech by making the physical
being express gravity and respect through study and
discussion--isn't this the way to make the physical
being conform to that of the sage?"[76]

This shows that in the mind of Ho Hsin-yin, a
man becomes a sage by studying and teaching. As
seen above, Ho felt that the focus of study--and
therefore the subject of teaching--ought to be the
actual occurrences within a person's realm of experience. An individual learns by experiencing
through his senses what is going on around him. Thus
Ho Hsin-yin stressed the learning process which takes
place through hearing. It should not be supposed,

however, that in speaking of this process Ho meant to
imply a one-way transmission of the truth from master
to pupil. Rather, in keeping with his faith in the
relationship between friend and friend, Ho envisioned
a reciprocal and dynamic relationship implying the
principle of equality with the participants contributing to each other's moral and intellectual development. That is, "it is possible for people to communicate with each other [as student and teacher]
without the student resting [permanently] in the position of student, and without the teacher resting
[permanently] in the position of teacher."[77]

Hence this relationship is best described as the
relationship between colleagues or associates. In
T'ai-chou theory and practice, they should activate
their common moral conscience by discussing the Way
of Heaven as it operates in the everyday world of
man. In terms of the community at large, this becomes a discussion among numbers of people where the
Way is discovered in the commonplace and comes to
life in the personal contact between participants.
This is why discussion (chiang) became the key concept in Ho Hsin-yin's philosophy of education: it
required face-to-face contact between people and involved the sort of interaction identified with friendship, based on the principles of equality and reciprocity. Chiang implies stimulating and, usually, am-

icable discourse with varying opinions offered and discussed, making learning a many-sided process in contrast to the one-sided process of learning of the self-taught and of the master-pupil relationship. Ho became such a vigorous advocate of public discussion in the independent academies because he saw this form of education as the only method of awakening the common people to their moral potential, their shared humanity. But its efficacy does not stem from the dialectical process alone; of equal importance is the level on which it is carried out. The teacher--the one who fully comprehends the Way--must be able to impart his ideas simply and clearly to reach the popular mind, enlightening even the humblest peasant to the truth within him, his share of the Way of Heaven. This is what Ho meant when he said that the "teacher makes learning simple and concise."[78]

When Ho Hsin-yin described studying and teaching as physical functions, he made sagehood available to all people, regardless of station in life, intellectual capacity, or scholastic training. It will be recalled that historically the sage was a member of the ruling class if not the ruler himself, combining both political and intellectual functions in society. As king, he was a model teacher insofar as he was a model ruler; he learned the lessons of the past and taught his subjects and successors by the example of his own exemplary behavior. As a scholar-official learned in the texts and histories recording the events of the past, the model Confucian advised his king and carried out the imperial will. Ho Hsin-yin acknowledged this tradition when he described the relationship between Yao and Shun, King Wen and King Wu, and King Wu and the Duke of Chou--all model rulers and ministers out of antiquity--as the reciprocal student-teacher relationship. He did this in a lengthy and at times obscure passage best quoted in its entirety and then explained.

> Yao and Shun were a sovereign and minister who were also student and teacher to each other. A commitment being made by Yao, it was honored by Shun. They were not committed differently. King Wen and King Wu were a father and son who were also student and teacher to each other. A commitment being made by Wen, it was honored by Wu. They were not committed differently. King Wu and the Duke of Chou were elder brother and younger brother who were also teacher and student to each other. A commitment being made by King Wu, it was honored by the Duke of Chou. They were not committed differently. . . .
>
> Although Wen and Wu were father and son, they were teacher and student to each other only in their capacities as sovereign and minister. Although King Wu and the Duke of Chou were elder and younger brother, they were teacher and student to each other

only in their capacities as sovereign and
minister. Their commitment was simply that
of sovereign and minister. There were no
other commitments. When it is considered
that Ku Sou was Shun's father and that Hsiang
was his younger [half] brother; and when it
is considered that Tan Chu was Yao's son and
that Shang Chün was Shun's son, and that Kuan-
shu and Ts'ai-shu were brothers of the Duke
of Chou, it appears that they [--Yao, Shun and
the Duke of Chou--] were committed to two
different ideals, but they were not. Though
Yao and Shun at first were [apparently] committed to two ideals, in the end there was only
one. Though the Duke of Chou at first was
[apparently] committed to two ideals, in the
final analysis, he had but one. The reason
that Shun caused a transformation [of Ku Sou
and Hsiang] and made them conform [to his
virtue] was that he was singly committed [to
the welfare of the realm]. The reason that
the Duke of Chou caused the execution of
[Kuan-shu and exiled Ts'ai-shu] and brought
about conformity was that he was singly committed [to the welfare of the realm].[79]

What is important here is the total commitment
of the sage, politically and morally, to the welfare of the realm. The men described became student and teacher to each other only as they were
related as sovereign and minister, regardless of
blood ties. The common commitment inculcated by
the student-teacher relationship transcends the

family: it is not a commitment to filial piety or
brotherly love and can only be fulfilled by those
whose responsibilities are to all men as, for example, were those of Yao and Shun. They were concerned above all else with their responsibility to
govern the country well. All other considerations,
including family ties, were subordinated to this
ideal. When a conflict arose between one's family
and his responsibility to the realm, the realm took
precedence. If Shun appears to have been moved by
consideration for his family in showing kindness toward his father and brother after they had conspired
against him, it was because he knew that by changing
Ku Sou and Hsiang for the good by the example of his
own exemplary behavior, he would prove himself to be
a model ruler, and the entire kingdom would be trans-
formed.[80] More importantly, Shun clearly placed
realm over family when he followed the precedent set
by Yao and passed over his own son to select Yü as
his successor.[81] When Ho said that the Duke of Chou
seems to have been doubly committed, he was alluding
to the Duke's service to King Wu and Wu's young son.
Both were relatives of the Duke--elder brother and
nephew respectively--but Ho clearly felt that he
assisted them because of their imperial positions
and his own responsibility to instill in them the
virtues of the model ruler. In Ho's mind the Duke

proved that his commitment was to the realm when he disposed of his own brothers as threats to the security of the country after they questioned his motives in acting as regent to his young nephew.[82]

Thus Ho Hsin-yin honored Yao, Shun, Wen, Wu, and the Duke of Chou as model rulers, statesmen, and teachers whose moral commitment extended equally to all men. At the same time, Ho made it clear that to him the implications of the student-teacher relationship are too great to be realized within the narrow relationship of parent and child or of brother and brother. But the intellectual role which Ho ascribes here to these men when he calls them students and teachers is vague at best. However, what is implicit here becomes explicit elsewhere. In citing the cases of Yao and Shun ignoring their own offspring in search of a successor to the throne, Ho suggested that the commitment of the sage not only transcends family barriers, but cuts across the barrier of time as well. Yao and Shun had learned the Way from their predecessor and were duty bound to find someone worthy of being taught and capable of carrying out the Way in years to come. In drawing attention to this aspect of the lives of sage-kings of old, he laid specific stress on their roles as model teachers in the world. For example, speaking of the learning of the sage, Ho said:

Yao passed it on to Shun and Shun passed it
on to Yü. They accumulated learning one
from another by holding fast to the Mean
and by being discriminating and of singular
purpose in it, studying it thus; and they
transmitted it one to another by making it
known through their expressions of admiration
and approval [of good qualities] and dissatisfaction and disapproval [of lesser
ones], discussing it thus. Sage after sage
transmitted learning one to another because
[succeeding] sages inherited it. Yü inherited
it from Shun after Shun had inherited it from
Yao. They made learning known one to another
through their expressions of admiration and
approval [of good qualities] and dissatisfaction and disapproval [of lesser ones], discussing it thus; and their successors inherited it one from another, accumulating
learning by holding fast to the Mean and by
being discriminating and of singular purpose
in it, studying it thus. Sage after sage
inherited learning because [preceding] sages
transmitted it. It was transmitted by discussion and inherited by studying.[83]

In other words, as described by Ho, the sages
of old functioned as teachers insofar as they taught
the Way of the sage to another member of the ruling
class. The recipient of this sort of teaching could
be an immediate successor, a reigning monarch being
tutored by a minister, or a minister being admonished
by his sovereign. And for all of these the ultimate
source of learning was the past as represented by

earlier sage-rulers. This is how the concept of the human ideal was preserved in the world and passed along over the ages from the time of Fu Hsi through the early years of the Western Chou Dynasty. Specifically, Ho gave credit for learning, practicing, and transmitting the Way of the sage in this manner to such eminent rulers and statesmen out of legend and history as Fu Hsi, Yao, Shun, Yü, T'ang and his chief minister I Yin, Kao Tsung and his prime minister Fu Yüeh, King Wu and his advisor the Viscount of Chi, and King Wen and the Duke of Chou.[84] Ho further said that what these men believed and taught is contained in the Book of Changes and in the "Great Plan" segment of the Book of History. He counted all but T'ang, I Yin, Kao Tsung, and Fu Yüeh among the authors of the Book of Changes and "Great Plan" and said that these four men learned the Way of the sage by studying these texts.[85] In accordance with the traditionally accepted view, Ho said that the Book of Changes originated with Fu Hsi and was amplified by King Wen and the Duke of Chou.[86] Also following tradition, Ho gave credit to Yü for formulating the "Great Plan" and said that the Viscount of Chi passed it on to King Wu.[87] And as described by Ho, consonant with the positions of these men, there evolved in both texts the concept of a political-intellectual elite as the guardian of all the world.

According to this notion social order is contingent
upon the moral welfare of the scholar-statesmen re-
siding at the topmost level of society, the object
of love and respect of all beneath him. Ho said that
in the Book of Changes put together by Fu Hsi, King
Wen, and the Duke of Chou, he is the sovereign
(chün^{bs});[88] and in the "Great Plan" of Yü, King Wu,
and the Viscount of Chi, he is the king (wang^{bt}).[89]

So to Ho Hsin-yin, during the Three Dynasties
period of Chinese history, the picture of the sage
was of a political and intellectual leader of society. To the extent that they achieved in their
lives what they considered to be the human ideal, Ho
honored the sage-kings of that time; as seen above,
he respected them as model and impartial rulers.
But he was convinced that there is inherent in all
things a principle more fundamental than even they
had realized. Or if they did realize it, they were
unable to teach it to others. It may be recalled
that Ho defined the true teacher as one who comprehends fully the Way of Heaven and is able to lead all
others to it with his simple and concise teaching.
But Ho lamented that both Fu Hsi and Yü lacked per-
ception in studying and clarity in teaching and that
even though kings Wen and Wu, the Viscount of Chi,
and the Duke of Chou were perceptive, they, too,
lacked clarity in their teaching.[90] That is, re-

gardless of whether or not they themselves had a clear idea of the Way of Heaven, the sage-rulers and sage-ministers of old were unable to teach it to the common people. In contrast, Ho described Confucius as a man who was able to teach clearly what he had learned. It was Confucius, he said, who completed for all the people in the world the story of what it means to achieve sagehood. Hitherto, as told in the Book of Changes and in the "Great Plan," this had been a story whose ending was known only to those who wrote it. But "Confucius completed what was left incomplete in the Book of Changes by studying it and teaching about it in the Ten Wings [to the Book of Changes] and in the twenty chapters [of The Analects], fulfilling in humanity (jen) what was achieved by Creative Power (yüan^{bu}) in the Book of Changes."[91] Confucius also gave a full explanation in the Ten Wings and in The Analects to what Yü, King Wu, and the Viscount of Chi left unclear in the "Great Plan," with the result that he "fulfilled in humanity (jen) what was accomplished by the sage in the 'Great Plan.'"[92]

Of primary importance here is that Confucius was a common man without official position or political responsibility. As seen above, Ho defined humanity as the mark of the true man among men. The love and respect of the true man extend directly to

all people within the realm of his experience, ben-
efiting them morally and materially. Appropriately,
Ho said that this principle was first enunciated in
the world by one who lived among the common people
as a teacher. Moreover, Confucius taught in such a
way as to enable the ultimate virtues of the Book of
Changes and of the "Great Plan" to be understood by
all the people. It is true that the scholar-statesmen had been concerned with the welfare of the people
and that Ho Hsin-yin had called them teachers. But
they lived above, not truly among, the people, and
as teachers they directed their efforts toward an
audience of the elite. What was taught the people
was taught by the example of model rulers and ministers. Confucius, on the other hand, aimed his
teaching directly at the common people. Consistent
with what he said elsewhere about studying the affairs of the world to comprehend the correct principle of things, Ho stressed that by discussing with
his listeners matters of everyday concern, Confucius
aroused their consciences and evoked their innate
quality of humanity. "There was not one affair
(shih) that was not studied and discussed by Confucius with his disciples Yen Yüan, Tseng Shen, and
others."[93] Further, "when Confucius studied and
taught about affairs together with his disciples Yen
Yüan, Tseng Shen and others, he was studying and

teaching about humanity, and he aroused humanity by studying affairs and by teaching about them."[94]

According to Ho Hsin-yin, this is how Confucius formed a school of like-minded men to teach and lead others. It was not a school based on broad learning and literary talents, but men of that bent were not excluded. The touchstone of the school was humanity, and its goal was to keep humanity alive in the world by awakening men to their own inner qualities. As if to justify his own readiness to meet with such men as Juan Chung-ho,[95] Ho stressed the universality of Confucius' school. Because humanity knows no bounds and is in us all, Confucius' teaching could appeal to men of such diverse character as Yang Chu and Mo Ti[96] As Ho put it: "In giving prominence to his school by studying and discussing humanity, Confucius did not limit his school to the literati (Ju[bv]) . . . . But he did cause such men as literati. . . to conform to humanity. . . so that for ten-thousand generations there would be literati to cause such men as Yang Chu and Mo Ti to conform. . . to Confucius' humanity."[97]

It may be said, then, that Ho Hsin-yin considered Confucius to be the archetype of the teacher of men: one who comprehends the Way of Heaven and is able to lead others to it. He was a sage embodying the principle of humanity among the common people. His commitment was to all the people of all times. Here was someone Ho could strive to emulate. He saw little in the sage-kings and their ministers that appealed to him personally. The idea of devoting the better part of his lifetime to books in order to become a minister of state repelled him. By its very nature the officialdom violated his sense of the equality of men and offered him no promise of security. However, this does not mean that Ho denied that sage-king his rightful place in the world. It means instead that while he admitted the vital role of the political leaders within society, he claimed a role of at least equal importance for the intellectual leaders, set apart in his mind from the ruler and officials. In looking back over history, Ho saw the emergence of what he defined as distinct but complementary functions of sages at two levels of society: the political function of the model statesmen--ruler and minister--exemplified by Yao and Shun; and the intellectual function of the model teacher exemplified by Confucius (with his disciples described as "friends" or "colleagues" yu-p'eng[bw]). In Ho's own words:

> The fulfillment of the Way starts above
> with the relationship between ruler and
> minister and is completed below with the
> relationship between friend and friend.

When there is communication between those
above and those below, the Way of father
and son, elder and younger brother and
husband and wife is unified and fulfilled
between them. The relationship between
father and son, elder and younger brother
and husband and wife are essential to the
fulfillment of the Way in the land, but
cannot unify all-under-Heaven. Only the
ruler and minister can gather together
the heroes of the land, govern according
to the principle of humanity, and thus make
humanity extend to all-under-Heaven. Are
the ruler and minister not responsible
for unifying all-under-Heaven? . . . [On
the other hand,] only through the relationship of friend and friend can the brave
and talented of the land be gathered together to establish a teaching in accord
with the principle of humanity, and make
all-under-Heaven return to it. [Thus]
is not the relationship between friend and
friend also responsible for unifying the
world? . . . If the teaching established
through the relationship between friend
and friend does not exist below, the Way
of the sage sovereign and minister will
not be made plain to the ten thousand
generations of the future. When the
sovereign and minister do not govern
[according to the principle of humanity]
above, the Way appropriate to the relationship between friend and friend cannot
be carried out. Thus are not the responsibilities of sovereign and minister and
friend and friend interdependent?[98]

In other words, to Ho Hsin-yin social harmony ultimately depends on the cooperation between the ruling class at the upper level of society and a community of teachers at the lower level. This idea is best understood against the background of Ho's other writings and his actual experiences. By stressing that self-fulfillment can only be achieved in the social context and that the man of humanity is a man among men, Ho made the individual potentially subject to any measures--positive or negative--deemed necessary by the government to insure order in human relations. This is particularly true of scholars and teachers who, like Ho himself, exist outside the ruling class and whose goal is to influence the minds of men. Teachers who support the official line are in turn supported by the government. Those who teach something other than what is officially sanctioned may be tolerated so long as they do not undermine the well being of the realm. But those who pose a direct threat to peace and order (in fact or in the mind of someone in high office) suffer immediate reprisals. Because Ho was an active dissenter as well as an outspoken adherent to a form of intellectual activity distasteful to some high officials, he learned firsthand to what extent authorities would go to enforce their own notion of orthodoxy. At the same time, however, in spite of

his own aversion to entering the bureaucracy, he
came to appreciate the need for cooperation with
officials. He engaged in active dissent at least as
early as 1559, when he opposed the special tax in
Yung-feng, and continued to oppose what he considered to be evil influences in government--mostly notably Yen Sung and Chang Chü-cheng--until his last
days. As a consequence he was arrested and exiled
in 1559, harrassed by Yen Sung's henchmen in the early 1560's and by government troops in the late
1570's. But highly placed friends gained his release
from exile, protected him from the Yen Sung clique
and helped him avoid arrest for almost three years.

What is important here is the lesson learned
early by Ho Hsin-yin that a man can assert his independence of the restrictions imposed by the official bureaucracy on its members simply by declining
to join it, but being a social animal, he cannot escape the actual existence of the ruling class itself. He is affected daily by the government's laws
and policies and cannot ignore them. If he finds
them distasteful, his alternatives are three: to
bear up under them, to seek a redress of grievances,
or to violate them. However, to anyone actively committed to the welfare of all men and to teaching and
leading them--that is, Ho's model teacher--only the
latter two alternatives are valid. Self-fulfillment

means to fulfill one's commitments to others. To live passively under an oppressive government is to fail others and, therefore, oneself. But in Ho's day a dissenting teacher could not stand alone against his oppressors, for as one who had rejected the official line--the very basis for all government action--his dissent represented a threat to the security of the ruling class (or to a vested interest group therein). He was thus likely to lose his freedom or, most probably, his life; and in either case it would obviously be impossible to carry on the work of Confucius. Therefore, in order to protect himself and his work (and, perhaps, to achieve self-fulfillment), it was necessary for Ho to form an alliance with like-minded officials from within the ruling class. These men were bound together by a common moral sense--more specifically, the feeling of humanity--and formed a community of interests. Practically speaking, this meant that the official provided Ho with a forum for giving his lectures, and Ho in turn made the official's task easier by awakening the sense of humanity in the people.

But during Ho's lifetime this sort of cooperation only occurred on a small, local scale. Ch'eng Hsüeh-yen could argue Ho's case in 1559, and Ch'eng Hsüeh-po could put him up in 1565; but no one could prevent Yen Sung's henchmen from harassing Ho for

several years after he helped impeach Yen in 1560,
nor was it possible to shield Ho entirely from the
attempts to arrest him after 1576. Similarly, Ho
could teach in Hsiao-kan and could even assist
Ch'eng Hsüeh-po in putting down the rebellion in
Ch'ung-ch'ing, but neither Ho nor his friends were
free to hold public philosophical discussion in or
near Peking; as seen in Ho's biography, Lo Ju-fang
was dismissed from office in 1577 for trying. In
short, Ho's friends and sympathizers within the official class were exceptions to the rule, and he
could only conclude that the actual holders of power
were diametrically opposed to his view of things.

As seen above, Ho Hsin-yin believed that social
order and justice are contingent upon government and
teachers being united in purpose by a common commitment to the principle of humanity. Of particular
significance here is the implication of official
recognition of what Ho considered to be the rightful
place in society of the academies and public philosophical discussion. For Ho Hsin-yin to say specifically that the rulers should govern in accord with
the principle of humanity is to say that the role
of government is to provide for the welfare and personal fulfillment of all people. Ho was convinced
that self-perfection can only be achieved in the relationship of friend and friend, understood by him

to be the reciprocal relationship between men engaged in open philosophical discussion. As student
and teacher to each other, these men achieve oneness
with the Way of Heaven and therefore become aware
of the innate moral sense common to all men. Reading from the specific to the general, as each individual perfects himself, the principle of humanity
governs all interhuman relations thereby insuring
permanent social order. It is therefore incumbent
upon any government concerned with the welfare of
the realm and the people in it to permit the teachers who comprehend the Way of Heaven to carry on the
work of Confucius and cover the land with the doctrine of humanity by holding public philosophical
discussion.

These, then, are the respective roles of the
model statesman and the model teacher in Ho Hsin-
yin's scheme of things. Both function according to
the principle of humanity, but they respond differ-
ently to the problems in the world. The statesman
fulfills his commitment to man and society by ac-
ceding to the role of the teacher and allowing him
to carry on his work. That is to say, the man holding political power does not exert himself to prevent a teacher from conducting lectures and awakening the people to the principle of humanity. It is
up to the teacher, on the other hand, to persist in

spreading the doctrine of humanity over the realm
and in establishing it firmly enough in the minds
of men as to enable it to withstand the pressures of
time. Thus did Ho Hsin-yin declare that without the
teacher the Way of the model statesman--that is, hu-
manity--would be lost. For the statesman to conduct
himself according to the principle of humanity is to
adhere to the rule of nonassertion. But someone outside of officialdom who comprehends the Way of Heav-
en and the implications of the principle of humanity
must actively participate in the social enterprise
to awaken the rest of the people, now and in the future, to the Way. This was the role of Confucius
and continues to be the role of all who follow in
his footsteps. Thus in the manner of <u>yin</u> and <u>yang</u>[bx] --
the complementary passive and active elements which
make up all things in the natural world--the model
statesman and model teacher complement each other
to bring order to the world of man.

The notion of official nonintervention in the
affairs of the people has its roots deep in the experiences of Ho's life. He was a frequent witness
to official behavior born out of self-interest and
not out of any consideration for the welfare of the
people. He saw local officials toady to their su-
periors and may well have been betrayed by men of
lesser rank bent on currying the favor of Chang Chü-

cheng. Worst of all, there were Yen Sung and Chang
Chü-cheng themselves, men of great power within official circles who, in Ho's view, were leading the
people astray. If the political leaders are of such
caliber, thought Ho, better that they do not meddle
in the affairs of the people. But if there was a
tendency among some officials toward self-aggrandizement, it should not be attributed solely to a weak-
ness in the makeup of the individual. For even high
minded officials of Ho's time failed to right the social wrongs which he felt were plaguing the people.
As explained by Ho, all of this was a manifestation
of the limits imposed on a man's full moral development by the demands of an official career:

> Regardless of how lofty a man's talents are,
> if he is caught in the [official] trap, he
> cannot develop them beyond being a loyal,
> meritorious and resolute official. How can he
> nourish the Great Way? . . . No one has
> illustrated the Great Way in the world more than
> Confucius did when, during the Spring and
> Autumn period, he shared the duties of
> government by communicating in good faith
> with his friends. . . . Yao and Shun ex-
> hausted goodness when they founded the
> government. But Confucius carried goodness
> to new heights when he established his
> teaching and did not allow himself to
> become involved in government. To refrain
> from becoming involved in government is
> to be honored more highly than founding a

government. Thus to go out and follow
Confucius' footsteps, led by a commitment to the Great Way, is to render a
great service to one's government. [99]

This is a reiteration of the earlier point that
the virtue of the sage-kings was the virtue of the
ruling class alone. As applied to the ruling class
of Ho's time, this meant that the narrow limits of
the ruling elite imperiled the official's development as one who could meet the moral needs of the
people. He was isolated from the people, and even
though he upheld what were considered to be the right
principles of his position, he could not apply them
to the problems of everyday life. When he intervened
in the daily affairs of man, his measures either
blocked the fulfillment of the essential qualities
of human nature or, at best, fell short of allowing
them full expression. But anyone outside the official framework was not subject to its restrictions
and was free to develop his inborn moral sense as he
participated in society at the grass roots level.
Not only could he comprehend the Way of Heaven, he
could also transmit it to others. Once this was
done, the people could take as the principle of
right and wrong their own innate moral sense and not
externally imposed laws and edicts. Thus to Ho the
man who serves his government best is the teacher
who carries on the work of Confucius by illustrating

the Way of Heaven in the world.

It appears, then, that Ho's ideal was that the model teacher should illustrate the Way of Heaven so well as to make it unnecessary for sovereign and minister to concern themselves with actively governing society. This notion was reflected in Ho's writings and activities as early as 1553 when he took up the task of reorganizing his clan into a self-sufficient unit. Admittedly, the documents he wrote at that time outlining his plans for clan reorganization do not contain specific references to the Way of Heaven or to the principle of humanity which recur in his later written works. But the spirit is the same. As has been shown, Ho regarded the existing system of family relations as a source of stress and conflict in the world. Because man's experience is restricted by the narrow limits of the immediate family, said Ho, he falls victim to a feeling of exclusiveness. His love does not extend beyond the members of his immediate family, and as a result he is oblivious of the needs of other people. He is willing to expend his efforts and resources only to guarantee the welfare of his own family. In short, exclusiveness begets selfishness. He considers himself to be the steward of his family's possessions and is determined to protect and to increase them by fair means or foul. For example, he is reluctant to pay taxes and is quick to take advantage of a weaker neighbor to increase his holdings. As a result, it is necessary for the government to take stern measures to enforce tax laws and to punish offenders and to maintain peace and order among men.[100] In brief, as Ho Hsin-yin saw it in 1553, the government was obliged to exert itself in the affairs of men because of the detrimental effect the family institution had on man's behavior.

To rectify this, Ho set about re-educating his fellow clansmen, and anyone else who cared to participate, to accept a broader view of the world. He was the teacher and he taught his pupils to transcend the narrow limits of the family and to extend their consideration and affection to all men. But because the family had long been the center of man's life, selfishness was deeply ingrained in his psychological makeup. For this reason Ho included in his education process during those years a set of strict and arbitrary rules to suppress what to him were the exclusive feelings of affection between family members. For example, all offspring were made to live together in a centralized location apart from their families, and visits with their parents were strictly regulated. Matters normally taken up within the family, such as marriage, were decided upon by Ho Hsin-yin himself.[101] These stern measures and Ho's

own arrogation of power--both clearly at variance
with the objectives of his reforms--were to be eliminated as progress was made toward his goal of awakening his fellow clansmen to their innate moral sense
so long obscured by the existing institution of the
family.[102] As more and more of the functions hitherto
performed by the family were taken over by the clan
organization,[103] people would find security in equal
relations with people outside the family. Family
life would cease to be the sum total of their experience, and they would no longer judge things according to their impact on the welfare of the family.
Exclusiveness would give way to cooperation and selfishness to altruism. The property men once fought
to protect even from the tax collector because they
considered it to be theirs by birthright would be
shared with others. The very concept of birthright
would lose its relevance if men would cease clinging
to the family as the source of livelihood and realize that what they have, including life itself, is
theirs as a gift from the ruler. Once men accept
this, said Ho, they will gladly return a portion of
what they grow in the fields in gratitude for the
ruler's benevolence.[104] Hence Ho Hsin-yin was convinced as early as 1553 that provided the teacher
does his work well, men will live in harmony and
even pay their taxes without active intervention

from above.

It is for this reason that Ho honored Confucius more highly than Yao and Shun and prized the role of the model teacher above that of the model statesman. But when he said that the man who illustrates the Way of Heaven in the world renders a service to his sovereign and realm, he did not simply mean that the model teacher has a privileged role in bringing order to society. Rather, to Ho Hsin-yin service to the realm is an imperative in every man's efforts to fulfill himself. It has been shown elsewhere that in Ho's mind the individual can only fulfill himself in society. His own welfare is secure only to the extent that he contributes to the welfare of others. Of primary importance in this is the commitment of everyone who comprehends the Way of Heaven to lead others to it. But Ho also said that "anyone who does not render service to the government [by illustrating the Way in the world] cheats the sovereign. How can someone who cheats the sovereign be aware of the importance of illustrating the Great Way?"[105] More simply put, the man who does not illustrate the Way of Heaven in the world not only does a disservice to himself and his fellowmen, but to his sovereign and realm as well. Because people are the stuff of which the realm is made, the realm's welfare stems directly from the moral integrity of men in their re-

lations with each other. Therefore, the teacher's
commitment to all men is also his commitment to sovereign and realm, and he realizes his full moral potential only when he fulfills both. This is what Ho
meant when he said:

> To acquire the [right] man for the realm is
> called humanity. . . . When the [right] man
> is acquired for the aged, he gives them
> rest; . . . when he is acquired for the
> young, he gives them comfort. He will
> always be one of those whose relations
> with each other are as friend and friend
> (p'eng-yu ^{by}) . . . . For such men study
> together in order to give rest to the
> aged and comfort to the young, and their
> emolument is the return of the realm to
> humanity.[106]

In other words, to Ho Hsin-yin the right man for the
realm is the teacher who, in the manner of Confucius,
understands his commitment to look after the well-
being of the realm's subjects. This places him firmly within human society and identifies him as a man
who has a strong sense of moral commitment. And yet
in the passage just cited, Ho ascribed humanity--
that is, moral perfection--to his actions only as
they relate to the realm and not as they relate to
another individual. The full measure of the model
teacher is his commitment to work for the perfection
of every person in the realm.

In the final analysis, then, Ho Hsin-yin's pro-

cess of self-perfection starts in friendship, proceeds to the service of the sovereign and society,
and culminates in the cultivation of the essential
nature of man. This represents a significant departure from the belief which grew up within Confucianism during and after the Han Dynasty that filial piety is the root of all virtue. According to
this notion the world is the family writ large, and
the ruler is the father of all the people. Only
when one learns to serve his parents reverently and
obediently can he serve ruler and society properly
and therefore achieve self-fulfillment. As stated
in the Classic on Filial Piety (Hsiao-ching), which
became popular during the Han: "Filial piety is the
root of all virtue and the source of all teaching.
. . Filial piety reaches its culmination when one
establishes himself in the practice of the Way of
Heaven and makes his name famous to future generations in order to glorify his parents. Filial piety
starts with service to one's parents, proceeds to
the service of the sovereign, and reaches its completion in the establishment of the [true] self."[107]
For Ho Hsin-yin, on the other hand, friendship is
the basis for all virtue. Man comprehends the Way
of Heaven and develops his own inborn sense of what
is right through intercourse between friends. Thus
he serves ruler and society by extending his love

and consideration to all men. Finally, to Ho man's
commitment is to keep the principle of humanity, and
not his parent's name, alive in the world.

NOTES

1. Jung (ed.), HHYC, p. 1.5-6. Yüan-hsüeh yüan-
chiang. (Hereafter references to the Ho Hsin-yin chi
include the page number followed by a period and line
numbers). Here Ho Hsin-yin used terminology from
the second of the nine divisions of the "Great Plan"
segment of The Book of History. Because this portion
of the "Great Plan" is of central importance in Ho's
discussion of human nature, it is best to quote it in
its entirety: "Of the five vital-affairs (wu-shih^{bz}),
the first is called physical being (mao^{ca}); the
second, speech (yen^{cb}); the third, sight (shih^{cc});
the fourth, hearing (t'ing^{cd}); and the fifth, thought
(ssu^{ce}). [The moral attribute of] physical being is
called respectfulness; of speech, accordance with
what is right; of sight, clearness; of hearing,
perspicacity; and of thought, sagacity. Respectfulness becomes manifest as gravity; accordance with
what is right, as orderliness; clearness, as wisdom;
perspicacity, as deliberation; and sagacity, as sageliness." The Book of History, V. iv. 6. Adapted
from Legge (trans.), The Shoo King or The Book of
Historical Documents, III in The Chinese Classics,
326-327 (hereinafter cited as "Legge [trans.], The
Shoo King").

It should be noted that the term shih^{cf} is rendered "vital-affairs" in this context because it
refers specifically to something concerned with the
existence and activity of the physical self, something concerned with and manifesting life.

2. Jung (ed.), HHYC, p. 1.9-10. Yüan-hsüeh
yüan-chiang.

3. Jung (ed.), HHYC, p. 40.8. Kua yü. Alluding to Mencius, VIIB.xxiv.

4. Jung (ed.), HHYC, p. 42.5-6. Pien wu-yü.
Chou Tun-i said "the essential way [to become a sage]
is to achieve oneness [of mind]. By oneness is
meant the absence of desire (wu-yü^{cg})." T'ung-shu
(Taipei), 1966; Ssŭ-pu pei-yao ed.), 20/4b. Adapted
from de Bary, et al. (comps.), Sources, p. 515.

5. Jung (ed.), HHYC, p. 42.8. Pien wu-yü.
This is a point made repeatedly by Hsün-tzu. See,
for example, Burton Watson (trans.), Hsün-tzu:
Basic Writings (New York: 1963), p. 150.

6. Jung (ed.), HHYC, p. 42.8. Pien wu-yü.
Citing Mencius, VIIB.xxxv.

7. Jung (ed.), HHYC, p. 40.9-10. Kua yü.

8. Jung (ed.), HHYC, p. 42.8-9. Pien wu-yü.
Citing Mencius, VIA.x.

9. Jung (ed.), HHYC, p. 40.10,14. Kua yü.

10. The term rendered here as the verb "to
govern" is ch'eng^{ch}, the second definition for which
in Tz'u-hai is chih^{ci} (Tz'u-hai, I, 102), corroborated by the definition osameru^{cj} in the Dai Kanwa
jiten, I, 350.

11. Referring to The Book of Changes, App. V.i.
3.

12. Here taking ch'eng in the sense of yin^{ck},
"to rely on." See Tz'u-hai, I, 102.

13. Jung (ed.), HHYC, p. 19.9-12. Yüan-hsueh
yüan-chiang. Alluding to the Mencius, VIIB.xxiv;
and to The Book of History, V.iv.6.

14. The term rendered here as the verb "to
govern" is yü^{cl}, the third definition for which in
Tz'u-hai is chih (Tz'u-hai, I, 1112), corroborated
by the definition osameru in the Dai Kanwa jiten,
IV, 4290.

15. Here taking yü in the sense of yin (J.
yoru) "to rely on." See Dai Kanwa jiten, IV, 4290.

16. Jung (ed.), HHYC, pp. 19.15 - 20.2. Yüan-hsüeh yüan-chiang. Alluding to The Book of History, V.iv.6; and to the Mencius, VIIB.xxiv.

17. Jung (ed.), HHYC, p. 72.5. Chü-ho lao-lao wen.

18. Jung (ed.), HHYC, p. 72.5. Chü-ho lao-lao wen.

19. Jung (ed.), HHYC, p. 67.5. T'i jen wei chi jen.

20. Jung (ed.), HHYC, p. 67.6. T'i jen wei chi jen. Citing The Analects, VIII.vii.

21. Jung (ed.), HHYC, p. 13.11. Yüan-hsüeh yüan-chiang. Alluding to The Analects, XII.i.

22. Jung (ed.), HHYC, p. 13.13-14. Yüan-hsüeh yüan-chiang.

23. Jung (ed.), HHYC, p. 67.5. T'i jen wei chi jen.

24. Jung (ed.), HHYC, p. 31.5-6,8. Lun chung. See The Book of History, II.ii.2.xv. The term rendered "all-pervading" here is kuan^{cm}. Its original meaning was "a string of cash," then "to thread together." Ho Hsin-yin apparently intended to convey the latter meaning when he used the character in the essay "Lun chung" to define the moral mind as something shared in common by all men, and thus as something binding all men together.

The term tao-hsin , rendered here as "Moral Mind," is distinguished from jen-shin^{cn}, "the human mind," in The Book of History, II.ii.2.xv. The translation of the terms tao-hsin and jen-hsin follows that of Professor Wing-tsit Chan in A Sourcebook in Chinese Philosophy (Princeton, 1963), pp. 581, 586, 616.

25. Jung (ed.), HHYC, p. 31.10. Lun chung.

26. Jung (ed.), HHYC, p. 68.6-9. Chü-ho shuai-chiao. . . .

27. Jung (ed.), HHYC, p. 40.9. Kua yü.

28. Jung (ed.), HHYC, p. 31.9. Lun chung.

29. Jung (ed.), HHYC, p. 39.5-6. Tao hsüeh.

30. Jung (ed.), HHYC, p. 29.7-8. Lun ch'ien.

31. Citing The Book of Changes, App. II, Hex.
I: "The concealed dragon does not act; it is like
the element yang is concealed in the earth." Chou
I, I in Shih-san-ching chu-shu, 1/9.

32. Jung (ed.), HHYC, p. 29.8-9. Lun ch'ien.

33. Jung (ed.), HHYC, p. 30.13. Lun ch'ien.

34. For example, see Jung (ed.), HHYC, p. 83.
Citing Ho Hsin-yin's letter to Tsou Ho-shan.

35. Jung (ed.), HHYC, p. 54.7-10. Ta chan-
kuo . . . pu lo i-ch'i.

36. Alluding to The Great Learning, 4.

37. Jung (ed.), HHYC, p. 54.10-11. Ta chan-
kuo . . . pu lo i-ch'i. Alluding to Mencius, IIA.
ii. 13-14.

38. Mencius and Hsün-tzu had the common goal of
providing for the emotional and material well-being
of their fellow-men. See Mencius, VIIA.xxiii, and
Watson (trans.), Hsün-tzu, pp. 34 and 37.

39. Jung (ed.), HHYC, p. 72.6. Chü-ho lao-lao
wen.

40. Jung (ed.), HHYC, p. 72.7-8. Chü-ho lao-
lao wen. Citing Mencius, IB.v.4. See also The
Book of Poetry, III.iii.6.

41. See Mencius, IVA.i.5.

42. Jung (ed.), HHYC, p. 27.4-5. Jen i.

43. Jung (ed.), HHYC, p. 27.6-7. Jen i.

44. According to Li Chih, one of the most prevalent charges made against Ho Hsin-yin by his contemporaries was that he abandoned four of the five
Confucian relationships. This is discussed below.

45. The Analects, I.ii.2. Adapted from Legge (trans.), Analects, p. 139.

46. Mencius, IVA.xxvii. Adapted from Legge (trans.), Mencius, pp. 313-314.

47. Quoting Chan (trans.), Reflections, p. xxiii.

48. Quoting Chan (trans.), Instructions, p. 205.

49. Jung (ed.), HHYC, p. 28.6. Lun yu.

50. Jung (ed.), HHYC, p. 28.6. Lun yu.

51. Jung (ed.), HHYC, p. 68.6-9. Chü-ho shuai-chiao. . . .

52. Jung (ed.), HHYC, p. 70 passim. Chü-ho shuai-yang. . . .

53. Jung (ed.), HHYC, p. 70.8-9. Chü-ho shuai-yang. . . .

54. Jung (ed.), HHYC, p. 70.12-14. Chü-ho shuai-yang. . . .

55. Jung (ed.), HHYC, p. 48.4-5. Teng Tzu-chai shuo.

56. The Great Learning, 3. Adapted from Legge (trans.), The Great Learning, I of The Chinese Classics, 357.

57. The Great Learning, 4-5. Adapted from Legge (trans.), The Great Learning, pp. 357-359.

58. Jung (ed.), HHYC, pp. 33.14-15; 34.6. Chü.

59. Literally, "without sound and without smell." This is language from The Doctrine of the Mean, XXXIII.vi.

60. Jung (ed.), HHYC, p. 33.10-12. Chü. The term rendered "pattern" here is ko[co]. To Ho Hsin-yin, ko-wu[cp] meant "to make things conform to the proper patterns," or "to rectify things."

61. Jung (ed.), HHYC, p. 41.14. Yüan-ching.

62. Jung (ed.), HHYC, p. 34.6-7. Chü.

63. The term used here is y̲ǔan^{cq} of Y̲ǔan-
c̲h̲i̲a̲o̲^{cr} the highest level of Buddhist teaching. See
Junjiro Takakusu, T̲h̲e̲ E̲s̲s̲e̲n̲t̲i̲a̲l̲s̲ o̲f̲ B̲u̲d̲d̲h̲i̲s̲t̲ P̲h̲i̲l̲o̲s̲-
o̲p̲h̲y̲, (Honolulu, 1956; 3rd ed.). pp. 118, 133-134.

64. The term rendered "literati" here is J̲u̲^{cs},
a term of obscure origin that was applied generally
during the Chou Dynasty to those who possessed an
education and who were versed in the arts and in
ritual and ceremony. Confucius was the most famous
representative of this group, and since about the
third century B.C. the term has been customarily
used for members of the Confucian School. J̲u̲ is rendered "literati" rather than "Confucian" in this
essay because Ho Hsin-yin departed from custom and
drew a sharp distinction between Confucius and his
followers and the J̲u̲ of his own day. In one place
Ho specifically denied that Confucius had been a J̲u̲,
though he acknowledged that Confucius welcomed them
into his school as he welcomed all people. Elsewhere Ho identified the J̲u̲ with the tradition of
Fu Hsi, Yao, and Shun, and as will be seen shortly,
he argued that Confucius rose above that tradition.
Ho conceded that Confucius was able to attract some
J̲u̲ to his teachings, but as seen in the passage just
cited, he complained that the judgment of latter day
J̲u̲ had been clouded by exposure to the mysteries of
Taoism and Buddhism. The implication is that this
precluded an understanding of the principles taught
by Confucius. In the final analysis, Ho used the
term J̲u̲ to denote a group of learned and scholarly
men ideologically distinct from the followers of
Yang Chu, Mo Ti, and the Taoists and Buddhists but
hardly to be equated as a group with those who understood and followed the principles of Confucius.

For discussions of the term J̲u̲ and of the group

of men so denoted, see in English Creel, <u>Confucius</u>
<u>and</u> <u>the</u> <u>Chinese</u> <u>Way</u>, pp. 171-181; Fung Yu-lan, <u>His-</u>
<u>tory</u> <u>of</u> <u>Chinese</u> <u>Philosophy</u>, trans. D. Bodde (Prince-
ton, 1952; 2d ed.; 2 vols.), I, 48; Liu Wu-chi, <u>A</u>
<u>Short</u> <u>History</u> <u>of</u> <u>Confucian</u> <u>Philosophy</u> (n.p., n.d.),
pp. 14-17. In Chinese, see Fung Yu-lan, <u>Chung-kuo</u>
<u>che-hsüeh</u> <u>shih-pu</u> (Shanghai, 1938), pp. 1-61; and
Hu Shih , <u>Lun-hsüeh</u> <u>chin-chu</u> (Shanghai, 1935; 2
vols.), I, 3-81.

    65. Jung (ed.), <u>HHYC</u>, pp. 34.16 - 35.4,9,11.
Chü.

    66. Jung (ed.), <u>HHYC</u>, p. 37.1. Chü.

    67. Jung (ed.), <u>HHYC</u>, p. 37.3. Chü.

    68. Jung (ed.), <u>HHYC</u>, p. 37.2. Chü.

    69. Jung (ed.), <u>HHYC</u>, p. 28.4. Lun yu.

    70. Jung (ed.), <u>HHYC</u>, p. 27.11-13. Shih shuo.

    71. Jung (ed.), <u>HHYC</u>, p. 1.4. Yüan-hsüeh yüan-
chiang.

    72. Jung (ed.), <u>HHYC</u>, p. 1.8. Yüan-hsüeh yüan-
chiang.

    73. Jung (ed.), <u>HHYC</u>, p. 1.11. Yüan-hsüeh
yüan-chiang.

    74. Jung (ed.), <u>HHYC</u>, p. 4.1-3. Yüan-hsüeh
yüan-chiang.

    75. Jung (ed.), <u>HHYC</u>, p. 4.5-7. Yüan-hsüeh
yüan-chiang.

    76. Jung (ed.), <u>HHYC</u>, p. 2.3-4. Yüan-hsüeh
yüan-chiang.

    77. Jung (ed.), <u>HHYC</u>, p. 28.1. Shih shuo.

    78. Jung (ed.), <u>HHYC</u>, p. 27.11. Shih shuo.

    79. Jung (ed.), <u>HHYC</u>, pp. 37.12 - 38.2. Tsung-
chih. According to tradition Yao ascended the
throne in 2357 B.C. and abdicated to Shun in 2255
B.C., who in turn descended in favor of Yü in 2205
B.C. Yao and Shun were the last of the so-called
Five Emperors, and Yü founded the legendary first

dynasty in Chinese history, the Hsia. King Wen was king of the principality of Chou during the last years of the Shang Dynasty, the first historical dynasty. His son King Wu overthrew the Shang and founded the Chou Dynasty. The Duke of Chou was King Wu's brother, and served as regent when the King's young son succeeded him. (All dates given above are according to the traditional Chinese method of reckoning.)

80. Shun's father and half brother made at least two attempts on his life. He survived both attempts to kill him, and even though he was aware of the guilt of Ku Sou and Hsiang, he was conciliatory toward both. Ho clearly did not ascribe this forgiveness to blood ties. See _Mencius_, VA.ii-iv.

81. When searching for a successor, Yao passed over his own son Tan Chu in favor of Shun because Tan Chu was "insincere and quarrelsome" (_The Book of History_, I.iii.9). Shun likewise disregarded his son Shang Chün as a successor and selected Yü. _Mencius_, VA.vi.1-2.

82. _Kuan_ is the name of a city that formed the appanage of Hsien , an elder brother of the Duke of Chou, whose historical name has become Kuan-shu. Similarly, _Ts'ai_ is the name of a small district that formed the appanage of Tu , younger brother of the Duke; and Ts'ai-shu has become his historical name. When King Wu, elder brother of all three men, died, the Duke of Chou became regent to Wu's young son Sung (known historically as Ch'eng). Acting out of envy, Kuan-shu "and his younger brothers" conspired against both the young ruler and the Duke. In retaliation, the Duke had Kuan-shu put to death and Ts'ai-shu exiled. _The Book of History_, V.vi.12; V.xvii.i.

83. Jung (ed.), HHYC, p. 6.1-4. Yüan-hsüeh yüan-chiang. In this passage Ho Hsin-yin alluded to the incident in The Book of History when Yao, in search of a successor, expressed his dissatisfaction with the qualities and talents of all candidates but Shun. Ho interpreted this to be a subtle method of transmitting the principles of the sage-king. According to this the enthroned sage-king revealed what he had learned to be the qualities of the sage by expressing approval of the qualities of the man he had chosen to succeed him. See The Book of History, I.iii.10-12.

84. Yao, Shun, Yü, I Yin, Kings Wen and Wu, and the Duke of Chou have already been identified. Fu Hsi, traditionally dated 2852 B. C., was the first of the Five Emperors and is said to have taught the people to hunt, fish, keep flocks, and make musical instruments. T'ang, known in history as T'ang the Completer, ascended the throne in 1766 B. C. and died in 1733 B. C. according to the traditional system of dating. Kao Tsung (Emperor Wu Ting) ascended the throne in 1328 B. C. and is credited with arresting for a time the decline of the House of Shang. (Mencius, IIA.i.8) On Fü Yüeh see The Book of History, IV.viii, Kao Tsung's charge to Fu Yüeh on his appointment to be prime minister. The Viscount of Chi is looked upon as one of the great paragons of virtue of the Shang Dynasty. He was an uncle and critic of the infamous last ruler of the Shang, who imprisoned him. Though released by King Wu, founder of the Chou Dynasty, the Viscount of Chi was reluctant to serve any dynasty but the Shang and agreed to become an advisor to Wu only after considerable hesitation. The Book of History, Preface 35; V.iii.9; V.iv.1-3.

85. Jung (ed.), HHYC, pp. 6.16-7.1; 7.13. Yüan-hsüeh yüan-chiang.

86. Jung (ed.), HHYC, p. 8.2-4. Yüan-hsüeh yüan-chiang. Ho Hsin-yin followed the traditional view that the eight trigrams were invented by Fu Hsi, the sixty-four hexagrams were formulated by King Wen, and the explanation of each horizontal line of each hexagram was composed by the Duke of Chou. See Legge (trans.), I Ching, pp. 6, 10.

87. Jung (ed.), HHYC, p. 4.15. Yüan-hsüeh yüan-chiang. According to Ho Hsin-yin: "The 'Great Plan' which was put into proper order by Yü, was revealed to King Wu by the Viscount of Chi after the King had inquired about it." (Jung [ed.], HHYC, p. 4.15. Yüan-hsüeh yüan-chiang.) Ho gave more credit to Yü for the origin of the "Great Plan" than the Viscount of Chi did when, in response to Wu's question concerning the principle of government, he said "Heaven gave the 'Great Plan' with its Nine Divisions to Yü." (The Book of History, V.iv.3. Quoted from Legge [trans.], The Shoo King, p. 323.) Nonetheless the order of transmission is the same.

It should be noted that Ho Hsin-yin neither gave specific credit to Yao and Shun for contributing to the Book of Changes and "Great Plan" nor did he specifically exclude them from the list of contributors. Instead, he seemed to allow for their influence on Yü when he referred to the "Great Plan" of Yao, Shun, and Yü. Jung (ed.), HHYC, p. 7.13. Yüan-hsüeh yüan-chiang.

88. Jung (ed.), HHYC, p. 12.8-9. Yüan-hsüeh yüan-chiang. The Book of Changes is concerned with the moral welfare of the chün-tzu, symbolized by the dragon, to the Chinese the emblem of wisdom, sovereignty, and sagehood.

89. Jung (ed.), HHYC, p. 12.13-14. Yüan-hsüeh yüan-chiang. The "Great Plan" is devoted to the perfection of the sovereign, referred to as Huang^ct and Wang^cu. The Book of History, V.iv.9, 16.

90. Jung (ed.), HHYC, p. 8.12-13. Yüan-hsüeh yüan-chiang.

91. Jung (ed.), HHYC, pp. 10.16 - 11.1. Yüan-hsüeh yüan-chiang. Yüan is the first character in the explanation of the Ch'ien hexagram, the first hexagram in the Book of Changes. Ho Hsin-yin identi- fied it as the ultimate attribute in the Book of Changes when he said that: "The number nine re- presents the ultimate attribute in the I Ching. King Wen used Creative Power (yüan) for the number nine." (Jung [ed.], HHYC, p. 11.12. Yüan-hsüeh yüan-chiang.) The number nine is used to designate the unbroken or yang line in the hexagrams as op- posed to the broken or yin line, designated by the number six. The Ch'ien hexagram is composed entirely of yang lines, and Ho said that when King Wen used the character yüan--Creative Power--to describe the Ch'ien hexagram, he identified it with yang, the ac- tive element. It appears, then, that Ho defined Creative Power as the ultimate attribute in the Book of Changes because it implies activity, which he valued so highly. In addition, he seemed to be as- cribing the qualities of creativity and action to the principle of humanity when he said that Con- fucius' jen fulfilled the functions of King Wen's yüan.

Tradition has it that Confucius wrote the sup- plementary commentaries and appendices, known as the Ten Wings, to the Book of Changes (see Legge [trans.], I Ching, pp. xxxi-xxxiv). Ho Hsin-yin was in agree- ment with this traditional belief. The Analects is,

of course, composed of twenty chapters or books.
Humanity (jen) is one of the major topics of discussion in The Analects, but occupies less space in
the appendices to the Book of Changes and none at
all in the body of the Book of Changes.

92. Jung (ed.), HHYC, p. 11.6-7. Yüan-hsüeh
yüan-chiang. The sage, or, more precisely, sageliness, is the highest form of moral development in
the "Great Plan." Humanity does not appear in the
"Great Plan."

93. Jung (ed.), HHYC, p. 8.12. Yüan-hsüeh
yüan-chiang.

94. Jung (ed.), HHYC, p. 9.10-11. Yüan-hsüeh
yüan-chiang.

95. See Ho Hsin-yin's biography on Juan Chung-
ho.

96. Yang Chu espoused the doctrine of "every
man for himself," and Mo Ti, the doctrine of universal love. See Mencius, VIIA.xxvi.

97. Jung (ed.), HHYC, pp. 23.16-24.3. Yüan-
hsüeh yüan-chiang.

98. Jung (ed.), HHYC, p. 66.2-10. Yü Ai Leng-
ch'i shu.

99. Jung (ed.), HHYC, pp. 73.11-14, 74.2-4.
Yu Shang Hai-lou shu.

100. Jung (ed.), HHYC, p. 70 passim. Chü-ho
shuai-yang. . . .

101. Jung (ed.), HHYC, pp. 68.13-69.10. Chü-
ho shuai-chiao. . . .

102. Jung (ed.), HHYC, p. 69.6-7. Chü-ho shuai-
chiao. . . .

103. For example, capping, marriage, and the
provision of food and clothing. Jung (ed.), HHYC,
p. 69.7. Chü-ho shuai-chiao. . . .

104. Jung (ed.), HHYC, pp. 70-71 passim. Chü-

ho shuai-chiao. . . .

105. Jung (ed.), HHYC, p. 73.15. Yu Shang
Hai-lou shu.

106. Jung (ed.), HHYC, p. 67.10,11-12,14.
Tz'u T'ang K'o-ta k'uei.

107. Hsiao-ching, VIII in Shih-san-ching chu-
shu, 1/2-3. For a discussion of the political implications of this doctrine of filial piety during
the Han Dynasty, see de Bary, et al. (comps.),
Sources, pp. 185-186.

IV

CONCLUSION AND EVALUATION

Ho Hsin-yin regarded Confucianism more as a way of life than as an academic discipline after his exposure to the teaching of the T'ai-chou School in 1546. It is true, of course, that he believed strongly in the efficacy of education, particularly during the last two decades of his life, and that he was determined to serve mankind as a teacher. But his approach to learning stressed personal activity and the effect of native intelligence operating in everyday life, not the intellectual exertion and mental discipline of scholarly study. He studied the Confucian texts only to verify the truths he observed and experienced in the common occurrences of everyday life. As a teacher he was not interested in giving lessons in reading and writing, but in spreading the principles of Confucianism as Confucius had done.

But Ho Hsin-yin quickly realized that the established institutions of Ming society were at odds with those principles and impeded man's efforts to live in accordance with them. Specifically he singled out the family and the official bureaucracy as impediments to the fulfillment of one's responsibil-

ities to society at large. His attitude toward
these two institutions reflect tensions built into
Confucianism and brought to the fore by the conditions of Ming society. His portrayal of the narrow
family relationships as the cause of selfishness implies tension between the ritual rules of conduct
governing family relationships and man's attempts at
spiritual enlargement and self-transcendence. In
terms of the essential quality of humanity (jen),
this represents a conflict between the demands of
its particular and its universal aspects, and between man's limited responsibilities and his responsibilities to society at large.

In criticizing the official bureaucracy, Ho complained that its members formed an elite group too
far removed from the people to be able to tend to
their well-being. In addition, he said that officials were often too preoccupied with their own
personal careers to show any concern for the welfare
of society. This dual criticism of the official
class reflects the tensions traditionally felt by
the Confucian scholar between his elitist tendencies
and his egalitarian ideals, and between his sense of
mission to society and his dislike for careerism on
the part of men void of true Confucian moral value.

Of special importance here is Ho Hsin-yin's
reaction to the conflicts and tensions he felt in

the existing order. As seen above, one of the factors alienating scholars from society during the early Ming was the presence in the ruling class of men from lower segments of society. With some early Ming scholars, their elitism prevailed over their egalitarianism and sense of mission, and rather than serve in the government with men from lower social strata, they retired from public office. In contrast, Ho Hsin-yin was alienated from the ruling class precisely because his egalitarian ideals and sense of mission prevailed: he was convinced that the needs of the people at all levels of society could not properly be met by serving in the government. But his overriding sense of mission made it impossible for Ho to follow other alienated scholars into seclusion. If he could not serve the needs of the people as an official, he clearly could not serve them by retiring to his ancestral home to study and teach. Rather than extricate himself from the tensions of the existing order, he tried to resolve them through social reform, in this way to enable all men to fulfill their responsibilities to society at large.

This raises the question of Ho Hsin-yin's personal approach to social reform. The new turn Ho took in his approach to reform after 1559 reflects his emotional and spiritual growth and a subtle shift in his view of human nature. His emotional and spiritual growth is seen in the unlimited scope of his reform efforts during the 1560's and 1570's. Prior to 1559 his efforts had been limited to his hometown and, for the most part, to members of his own clan. By Ho's own account this was because of the teaching in the Great Learning that a well-ordered family is the basis of a well-ordered world. But an even more important factor that should not be overlooked when analyzing Ho's early efforts at reform is the importance of the kinship system to the Chinese. Ho was independent enough in 1553 to offer a new definition of interpersonal relationships within the clan organization, but he was not yet ready to forego the security of the clan itself. On the contrary, at this stage in his development his concern was the typically Chinese one of trying to increase the effectiveness of the clan in providing its members with security. In addition, it should be noted that information drawn from secondary sources and from Ho's own recollections indicate that he had little contact with the world outside Kiangsi Province until after he was forty years of age. His recorded travels prior to 1558 kept him in and about his native prefecture and the provincial capital area slightly to the north.

Such limited exposure to the outside world and to
the problems of its inhabitants would tend to rein-
force his ties with the area of his birth and to
intensify his feelings of concern for the problems
he found there.[1]

There is nothing to suggest that Ho had any inclination to return to Yung-feng after his release
from exile to continue his clan reform. Nor is there
evidence that he attempted local reforms or to establish collective communities elsewhere, even after
the threat from Yen Sung's followers had disappeared
and, from all indications, he was free to do as he
pleased. He took as his immediate concern during
the 1560's and 1570's, not simply a local community
nor his blood relatives, but mankind itself, ac-
cepting as his dependents the lowly, the powerless,
and the seemingly simple in mind. He now envisioned
a vast "family" encompassing all people and reaching
back to what he perceived as the beginning of the
Confucian School. This socially created family
tended to replace the biological family as Ho's focus of behavior. Ho's concerns and activities during the '60's and '70's suggest that he had gained
a broader perspective, a wider knowledge of society
and a deeper understanding of the magnitude of the
problem he was facing: the failure of society at
large to reflect the principles of Confucianism and

the suffering this caused, particularly among the common people.

The contrasting techniques Ho Hsin-yin employed before and after 1559 to alter existing institutions suggest a subtle philosophical shift concerning human nature and its role in perfecting society. Ho had always regarded man as a social animal, but during the 1550's he seemed reluctant to place full trust in human virtue as a force for social reform. The reform documents he made public in 1553 reveal a keen sense of awareness of the problems involved in trying to change patterns of behavior deeply ingrained in man's psychological makeup and reinforced by a long-established institutional structure. This awareness led Ho to adopt measures that were not totally Confucian in character. He acknowledged that men were educable, but he lacked full Confucian confidence that existing attitudes could be changed through education alone. He felt that he could teach people a new code of conduct based on his conception of fundamental Confucian principles, but he was not convinced that this knowledge would lead to a spontaneous change in their personal lives. For this reason, his reform program of the 1550's stressed the dual but complementary aspects of education and institutional restraint--education to inculcate the

new code of conduct and institutional restraint to
prevent return to old behavioral patterns. This
left little room for spontaneity but was based on
a realistic evaluation of human nature and of society.

Ho Hsin-yin's activities during the 1560's and
1570's suggest a more idealistic view of human nature and of social reform. During this period he
relied exclusively on education as an instrument of
reform. Eschewing techniques he used in Yung-feng
to suppress old habits and to enforce new ones, he
now sought through his public lectures to awaken
the people to their essential quality of humanity,
believing that once activated, this would inspire
men spontaneously to reject old patterns of behavior and to adopt new ones based on the principle
of "forming one body with all things." He was convinced that when people were inspired to moral action based on this principle, their deeds would
produce the new society he envisioned.

Regardless of what method Ho Hsin-yin used to
solve the problem of social change--whether by dic-
tating a new social blueprint or by educating the
people to make adjustments according to their own
moral consciences--it should be remembered that his
goal was always the same: to enable every individ-

ual to achieve his ultimate potential as a human being by fulfilling his sense of care and concern for all mankind. With Wang Ken, Ho Hsin-yin declared that all men have it within themselves to become sages and claimed for the common man the right of direct access to sagehood, regardless of status in society or intellectual achievement. In addition, Ho stayed well within the bounds of Confucian social thought during both stages of his career. There recur throughout his writings from both periods these cardinal Confucian principles: that to live in the world means to be a responsible man among men; that reciprocity is the basis of all social relations; and that all higher forms of social organization reflect the essential quality of lower forms and ultimately of human nature itself.

In the last analysis Ho Hsin-yin's efforts as a reformer were destined to fail because of his own audacious nature. Ho envisaged an active political role for himself in society. Education became a political activity for him when it became a force working to determine anew the structure of society and the proper relations between society and its members. He disagreed with accepted theory on how to maintain order and social harmony, had worked out a new one, and because he was convinced that those holding power could not or would not adminis-

ter it, was trying to rally the people to carry it
out themselves. In simplest terms, the lesson Ho
taught in the lecture halls was that he had a better method of running society than the one currently
being employed. This was the first point of conflict between Ho and the authorities. During the
Ming education had always been conceived of as a
conservative force, inculcating official orthodoxy
and providing men of unquestioned philosophical purity to staff the bureaucracy. But neither Ho's
unorthodox view of education nor the content of his
lectures was the main factor responsible for his
demise. Rather, that factor was his refusal as a
teacher to make concessions to the hard realities of
Ming political life. To Ho it was of the utmost importance personally and philosophically that he
"continue to exert effort with diligence" in the
manner of Confucius himself. Thus, even after two
attempts had been made to arrest him in the late
1570's he carried on as before, traveling about the
countryside and conducting public discussion in the
academies. And now, officially regarded as a fugitive, he could only compound the gravity of his
situation because the very act of conducting a public lecture constituted an act of defiance and political dissent. What ultimately sealed his fate,

then, was the militant rectitude he espoused--the
state of moral earnestness that he pursued with unrelenting passion until the moment of his death.

Ho's status as a fugitive after 1576, and his
refusal to desist from activities that might further
offend the authorities, had serious implications for
his friends on whom he had relied for support and
patronage since 1560. For them to continue to offer
aid and hospitality while he was a fugitive meant to
share in his defiance and dissent and to jeopardize
their own positions and security. Nonetheless,
there were those who remained steadfast in their support of Ho, warning him of impending arrest attempts,
traveling with him as he fled government troops, and
offering him sanctuary in their homes. There are re-
ports that at least one of these devoted friends
died for his efforts on Ho's behalf. On the other
hand, in an essay eulogizing Ho, Li Chih, one of
Ho's most ardent admirers, condemns as hypocrites
some of Ho's former associates for failing to act
to save him. Most harshly criticized by Li is Keng
Ting-hsiang, Ho's friend and T'ai-chou colleague
since 1560 and an influencial official at the time
of Ho's death. Keng played a prominent role as one
of Ho's patrons during the years when he was free
to roam the countryside and lecture in the academies,

but his name is notably absent from the accounts of the final, troubled years of Ho's life.

The literature written about Ho Hsin-yin by his contemporaries and by men of later times frequently contains unfair criticism of Ho and of his ideas. There are two main reasons for this. First, Ho's contemporaries could only judge him on the basis of what they saw and heard of his day-by-day activity, and when viewed out of context and not in the light of his philosophy and life as a whole, his behavior can leave a variety of impressions that are not always accurate. So some criticism of Ho contained in the literature of the Ming and Ch'ing could conceivably be the result of an honest misunderstanding of his motives and intentions. On the other hand, it is not unlikely that his enemies deliberately misrepresented Ho Hsin-yin in written documents, and that these documents later influenced historians writing about Ho. But whatever the cause, unfair criticism of Ho Hsin-yin does exist, and it should be analyzed in the light of what is now known of Ho's philosophy and life as a whole.

One charge made against Ho Hsin-yin that requires close scrutiny is that he discarded four of the five Confucian relationships, retaining only the relationship between friend and friend. According to Li Chih, this was one of the most prevalent

charges made against him by his contemporaries.[2]
It is true that Ho declared the right of every individual seeking self-fulfillment to assert his independence of the narrow family relationships and to
forego membership in the ruling class. And as seen
in his biography, Ho lived apart from his family for
the last twenty years of his life, and became an
outspoken critic of the bureaucratic establishment
and some of its members. On the other hand, it
should also be remembered that he returned to his
home while under threat of arrest to mourn the death
of his parents, and that he assisted a loyal official
in suppressing an insurrection against the throne.
But at best these episodes were exceptions to the
rule. It cannot be denied that in his personal life
Ho Hsin-yin devalued the importance of the family
and the ruling class and the relationships they com-
prised.

Ho's lifestyle should not be construed to mean
that the basic kinship and political relationships
had lost all significance for him, however. He was
disenchanted with those relationships as they existed
in his own day, but as a Confucian he could not ignore them. He spent vast amounts of moral and literary energy evaluating inter-personal relationships
in general, elucidating their relative strengths and
weaknesses as he perceived of them and explicating

his view of their proper roles in society. There
is ample evidence in his written works to show that
the family relationships and the relationship between ruler and minister were vital elements in his
social and political philosophy. In a passage already quoted in this study, Ho said that "the relationship between father and son, elder and younger
brother and husband and wife are essential to the
fulfillment of the Way in the world." In the same
passage he declared that "the fulfillment of the Way
starts above with the relationship between ruler and
minister," and added that "only the ruler and minister can gather together the heroes of the land,
govern according to the principle of humanity and
thus make humanity extend to all-under-Heaven." The
problem as Ho saw it was that these relationships
as they existed during the Ming impeded rather than
encouraged the expression of the Way and humanity in
the world. He argued that they interfered with a
person's relationship to society as a whole, that
demands made by the family and by an official career
distracted the individual from the broader responsibilities to all mankind. This criticism reflects
the traditional Confucian principle that a man should
not lose his identity as a true human being within
the family or in government service; that is, that

he should not allow family interests or career considerations to destroy his sense of unity with his
fellow human beings. Ho considered this to be the
most fundamental principle in the Confucian Classics,
and the desire to revive it was what motivated him
as a teacher and social reformer. But he concluded
from personal experience and observation that the
only way he could live according to that principle
in the meantime was to alter the relative importance
of the five relationships, making friendship the
most important relationship in his personal life.
He saw friendship as the only existing relationship
that inspired people to give full expression to their
humanity, enabling them to express love and respect
for each other, not because of common family ties,
status or occupation, but because of each person's
intrinsic worth as a human being. As a teacher
approaching others in the spirit of friendship, Ho's
objective was to awaken the people in their shared
humanity; and as a reformer, his objective was to
inspire the people to alter family relationships
and the relationship between ruler and minister so
that they would foster rather than impede the expression of humanity and the Way.

Among the charges made against Ho Hsin-yin by
late Ming and early Ch'ing authors, perhaps the most
serious from the standpoint of someone who consid-

ered himself to be a Confucian thinker was that he had lapsed into Ch'an Buddhism. This is the charge made by Huang Tsung-hsi in the brief introduction to his discussion of the T'ai-chou School in the Ming-ju hsüeh-an. Specifically, Huang said that Ho Hsin-yin had thrown the world into confusion by practicing the Ch'anist doctrine of "revealing the true nature through activity." He went on to say that when practiced by Ho this doctrine was more dangerous than when practiced by the Ch'an masters themselves. The latter were restrained in their behavior by their sense of proper timing. For example, they would strike or shout at a student to help induce enlightenment when the moment was right, but would restrain themselves at other times. In contrast, as Huang described Ho Hsin-yin and his followers, they lived the doctrine of self-assertion unrestrained by any sense of proper timing.[3]

Huang Tsung-hsi's impressions of Ho are not entirely unjustified. Ho Hsin-yin taught the interdependence of the moral and physical selves and that man expresses his moral qualities through physical activity. He believed as the Ch'an Buddhists did that one's true nature should be expressed immediately in the activities and experiences of everyday life. For Ho Hsin-yin personally this led to the doctrine of unrestrained self-assertion that he prac-

ticed in the extreme, particularly during the last
two decades of his life. But if this suggests some
similarities between Ho and the Ch'an Buddhists,
there is a crucial difference between them that shows
Ho to have a typical Confucian outlook and clearly
sets him apart from the Buddhists. The chief factor
distinguishing Ho Hsin-yin from the Ch'anists is his
recognition of the moral imperative as the basis for
personal cultivation. Ho adhered closely to the Confucian view of man that defines a person's true nature in terms of his relationship with other people,
a view that makes the fulfillment of the inescapable
moral obligations to other people and to society the
basis for the realization of the true nature. It
was this sense of moral obligation and the determina-
tion to fulfill it, in this way to develop his true
nature and therefore to realize his true potential,
that motivated Ho Hsin-yin to act as he did. The
Confucian process of personal cultivation demanded
that he assert himself to solve the problems of human society and to alleviate the suffering caused
by those problems. In contrast, according to the
Buddhists' view of man, this sense of personal attachment and moral obligation to society and its
members would prevent the realization of the true
nature. While the Confucian tried to refine his
sense of moral judgment--his sense of good and evil--

in order to serve good and eliminate evil, the Buddhist tried to achieve insights that rose above moral
judgments and considerations of good and evil. To
do this, the Buddhist had to free himself from attachment to and dependence upon external things or
ideas, including the natural human affections and
moral obligations of human relationships that were
so important to Ho Hsin-yin and to Confucians generally. In accordance with this Buddhist view, the
bodhisattva was under no obligation to try to solve
the problems of human society as Ho Hsin-yin was.
His primary concern and chief function was to enlighten others and to free them from attachment to
externals.

In addition to charging Ho Hsin-yin with Buddhist leanings, Huang Tsung-hsi also identified him
with a pair of fourth century B. C. political adven-
turers named Chang I^{cv} and Su Ch'in.^{4cw} For purposes
of comparison a few words should be said about the
lives of these two men. Chang I and Su Ch'in lived
during the so-called Warring States Period (fourth-
third centuries B. C.) when seven rival states were
vying for control of the territory nominally under
the jurisdiction of the Chou court. Before launching
separate careers as political advisers in first one
of the rival courts and then another, Chang I and
Su Ch'in studied together in the school of a Taoist

philosopher versed in the art of sophistical persuasion. After leaving his teacher, Su Ch'in's first stop was in the state of Ch'in where he tried to convince the king that he should attack his six rival states. After being rebuffed, he switched loyalties and changed his argument, and taking advantage of personal and local idiosyncracies he was able to persuade the rulers of the six anti-Ch'in states to form a confederacy against their common foe. In the obverse, after failing to make an impression in the state of Ch'u, a rival of the state of Ch'in, Chang I became minister to the Duke of Ch'in. In time he succeeded where Su Ch'in had failed and persuaded the Duke to move against the confederacy, and was instrumental in defeating the state of Ch'u.[5]

Briefly, Chang I and Su Ch'in can best be described as strategists who used questionable means to achieve more questionable ends. Huang Tsung-hsi was not entirely without justification in identifying Ho Hsin-yin with these two men. Such an identification has some basis in Ho's actual conduct, most notably in his participation in the plot against Yen Sung in 1561. When he joined the Taoist magician to undermine Yen Sung's reputation and career by deceiving the Emperor, Ho violated the Confucian principle that deception should not be used to influence the ruler[6] and made himself vulnerable to the criticism that he resorted to stratagem to achieve his goal. So on the surface, at least in the matter of his complicity with Lan Tao-hsing, it appears that Ho was culpable as an opportunist and that Huang Tsung-hsi was just in indicting him as such. On the other hand, Huang's indictment becomes less valid when viewed in the light of Ho's philosophy and life as a whole. This is what Shimada Kenji does in his <u>Chūgoku ni okeru kindai shii no zasetsu</u>. In this study Shimada discusses Ho Hsin-yin's personal approach to life in terms of his role as a hero or knight-errant in society. If one accepts the view that the goal of the Confucian is to conduct his life in accord with the Principle of Heaven (<u>t'ien-li</u>^{cx}) and to illustrate the Way without regard for stratagem or personal success, and the view that the knight-errant must rely on stratagem to succeed in the world, then it might appear that Ho Hsin-yin did not live up to the traditional notion of what Confucianism is and that Huang Tsung-hsi was correct in his judgment of Ho. But as Shimada correctly points out, Ho Hsin-yin stressed above all else the importance of conducting one's affairs in accord with the correct principle of things (<u>li</u>^{cy}) and to this extent adhered closely to the spirit of the traditional Confucian scholar. If he had to become a hero or knight-errant to inspire the people to accept his view of the correct principle as their standard of behavior, it was because he sensed that the conditions of society were opposed to it.[7]

The implications of Ho Hsin-yin's complicity with the Taoist magician Lan Tao-hsing go beyond Huang Tsung-hsi's criticism and involve another matter that was of more immediate concern to Ho. Ho acknowledged in letters written after his arrest in Ch'i-men that he had been accused of engaging in the arts of the magician.[8] In his own defense he argued that this accusation did not coincide with the facts of his life. He pointed out that one would expect a magician to use the language of magic, to perform deeds of magic, and to hold company with colleagues in the magical arts. But in recounting his life's story, Ho showed that he had traveled and lived with respected state officials and that in his teaching and lecturing he had stayed within the bounds of orthodox Confucianism.[9] But there is still the argument that Ho acted in league with the Taoist magician in Peking against Yen Sung. Due to the absence of corroborating evidence, however, and when viewed against the background of his full life's story, far from being proof that Ho was a magician himself, this episode becomes an example of his opposition to unjust officials, of his active concern

for the welfare of society, and of his willingness
to enlist anyone in his cause.

Ho Hsin-yin attracted little attention in modern scholarly circles until resurrected in the works
of scholars on the China mainland and in Japan.
Many of these twentieth-century students of Ho Hsin-
yin pay special attention to his social and political activities, laying particular stress on his collective view of society[10] and on his apparent opposition to the bureaucracy.[11] Special note should
be taken of the interpretation of Ho Hsin-yin's
ideas that appears in Hou Wai-lu's history of Chinese thought. After a competent and thoroughgoing
analysis of his life and thought, Hou discusses Ho
Hsin-yin's concepts of "humanity" and "righteousness" in materialist terms, saying that they should
not be understood in their abstract sense, but as
answering to the material demands of life. It is
true, of course, that Ho Hsin-yin was not interested
in humanity and righteousness--nor for that matter
in the Way of Heaven or principle--as abstractions,
but only as they are applicable to the everyday affairs of life. But it should not be forgotten that
when he discussed these concepts, Ho discussed them
in humanistic terms, stressing their moral and spiritual aspects and their applicability to the practical affairs of life to insure the moral and spiritu-

al welfare of men in their relationships with each
other.[12]

Because Ho Hsin-yin had little apparent effect
on the social and intellectual development of China,
there has been a tendency to disregard him (and other
T'ai-chou School men) when studying the Ming Dynasty.
This has led to a misunderstanding of Ming learning
and education. For example, Liang Ch'i-ch'ao im-
plied that it was in reaction to the speculative nature and excessive bookishness of Ming learning that
such Ch'ing scholars as Yen Yüan and Li Kung taught
that "knowledge should not be sought by introspec-
tion nor from books, but from daily activities."[13]
This statement might well be used to describe the
approach to learning taken by Ho Hsin-yin himself,
who used books, not as the primary source of knowledge, but to verify and document what he learned
from his daily experiences in the world. In addition, Liang said that during the Ming Dynasty "the
civil service examinations and students' curriculum
to prepare for them engaged the attention of all
the nation; students needed only to learn this kind
of dubious and imitative language in order to be
ready to jockey for position, wealth, and reputation. The whole nation indulged in it prodigally
and one man after another neglected his learning
and the use of his mind."[14] In other words Ming

learning and education were subordinated to official recruitment. This view ignores the efforts of Ho Hsin-yin. He sensed a moral vacuum in Ming society that could only be filled by a vibrant Confucianism attuned to the needs of men caught up in the rapid change of the sixteenth century. He was convinced that this could not be found within the state-operated schools, which prepared men for government service and taught them to manage their own affairs, but which hindered them from moral cultivation. He longed for a return to the simple, fundamental moral principles taught by Confucius to his followers and at the same time for a revival of the methods of education used by Confucius--a method of education unrelated to the state examination system.

In the final analysis, it can be said that Ho Hsin-yin represents both the instinct within Confucianism for active social endeavor, and the tendency among the Ming scholars to forego government service. Ho Hsin-yin's philosophy was one of involvement and total participation in the social enterprise. He had none of the contemplative bent that led even Wang Ken to combine the active life of the teacher with the life of meditation. In terms of Confucianism as both a doctrine of moral cultivation and a doctrine upholding a cultural tradition, he stressed the former in the extreme. To meet the needs of men caught up in the flux of a complex society, he reduced Confucianism to the fundamental principles of moral cultivation taught by Confucius. In so doing he located a common ground between the idealistic values of Confucian theory and the realistic needs of the Chinese people. This does not mean that he abandoned the ideal value system of the Confucian classics nor that he went beyond the basic orientation of society. He simply rearranged both so as to mitigate the tensions he experienced and perceived in everyday life.

NOTES

1. In contrast to Wang Ken, for example, who is known to have traveled widely with his father on business trips as a boy.

2. Jung (ed.), HHYC, Intro. p. 11. Citing Ho Hsin-yin lun. See Li Chih, Fen Shu, p. 89.

3. Huang, MJHA, VI, 32/62. T'ai-chou hsüeh-an.

4. Huang, MJHA, VI, 32/64. T'ai-chou hsüeh-an.

5. See Friedrich Hirth, The Ancient History of China (New York, 1923), pp. 307-314.

6. See The Analects, XIV.xxiii.

7. Shimada, Chūgoku ni okeru kindai shii no zasetsu, pp. 139-144. For another analysis of Huang Tsung-hsi's criticism of Ho Hsin-yin that is sympathetic to Ho, see Okada Takehiko, "Ō-mon genjōha no keitō ," Teoria , VIII (1965), 35.

8. See Jung (ed.), HHYC, pp. 77-79, 83. Citing Ch'i-men letter and letter to Tsou Ho-shan.

9. Jung (ed.), HHYC, pp. 77-79, 83. Citing Ch'i-men letter and the letter to Tsou Ho-shan.

10. See, for example, Hou, t'ung shih, IVB, 1018-1019; Jung (ed.), HHYC, Intro. p. 1; Jung, Ming-tai ssŭ-hsiang shih, pp. 223-224; and Ono Kazuko, "Jukyō no itansha tachi ," Taidō Suru Ajia , ed. Matsumoto Sannosuke (Tokyo, 1966), pp. 20-22.

11. Jung (ed.), HHYC, Intro. pp. 109.

12. Hou, t'ung-shih, IVB, 1022.

13. Liang Ch'i-ch'ao, Intellectual Trends in the Ch'ing Period, trans. Immanuel C. Y. Hsü (Cambridge, 1959), p. 22 (hereinafter cited as "Liang, Intellectual Trends").

14. Liang, Intellectual Trends, p. 28.

SELECTED BIBLIOGRAPHY

I. Primary Sources Relating to the
Life and Thought of Ho Hsin-yin

Ch'eng Hsüeh-po [程學博] Chi Liang Fu-shan hsien-sheng wen [祭梁夫山先生文], HHYC, pp. 135.8-137.5.

Ho Hsin-yin [何心隱]. "Chü"[矩], HHYC, pp. 33.9-37.7.

_____. "Chü-ho lao-lao wen" [聚和老老文], HHYC, p. 72.7-11.

_____. "Chü-ho shuai-chiao yü-tsu li-yü" [聚和率教諭族俚語], HHYC, pp. 70.1-71.16.

_____. "Chü-ho shuai-yang yü-tsu li yü" [聚和率養諭族俚語, HHYC, pp. 70.1-71.16.

_____. "Jen i" [仁義], HHYC, p. 27.1-9.

_____. "Kua yü" [寡欲], HHYC, pp. 40.7-41.2.

_____. "Lun ch'ien" [論潛], HHYC, pp. 29.7-31.3.

_____. "Lun chung" [論中], HHYC, pp. 31.4-33.8.

_____. "Lun yu" [論友], HHYC, p. 28.3-11.

_____. "Pien wu-yü" [辯無欲], HHYC, p. 42.4-12.

_____. Shang Ch'i-men Yao ta-yin shu [上祁門姚大尹書], HHYC, pp. 77.1-79.12.

_____. Shang Chu pa-tsung shu [上朱把總書],

HHYC, pp. 102.14-105.7.

_____. Shang Kan-chou Meng chün-men shu [上贛州蒙軍門書], HHYC, pp. 98.7-99.14.

_____. Shang Ling-pei tao-hsiang t'ai-kung-tsu shu [上嶺北道項太公祖書], HHYC, pp. 91.1-93.4.

_____. "Shih shuo" [師說], HHYC, pp. 27.10-28.2.

_____. "Ta chan-kuo chu-kung K'ung-men shih-ti chih yü chih pieh tsai lo i-ch'i yü pu lo i-ch'i" [答戰國諸公孔門師第之與之別在落意氣與不落意氣 , HHYC, pp. 54.6-55.14.

_____. "Tao hsüeh" [道學], HHYC, p. 39.4-9.

_____. "Teng Tzu-chai shuo" [鄧自齋說], HHYC, p. 48.1-12.

_____. "T'i jen wei chi jen" [題仁為己任], HHYC, p. 67.4-8.

_____. "Tsung-chih" [宗旨], HHYC, pp. 37.8-39.3.

_____. "Tz'u T'ang K'o-ta k'uei" [辭唐大可餽], HHYC, 67.9-68.1.

_____. Yü Ai Leng-ch'i shu [與艾冷溪書], HHYC, pp. 65.12-66.10.

_____. "Yü hui" [語會], HHYC, p. 28.3-11.

_____. Yu shang Hai-lou shu [又上海樓書], HHYC, pp. 73.10-74.4.

_____. Yu shang Kan-chou Meng chün-men shu [又上贛州蒙軍門書], HHYC, pp. 100.1-101.12.

_____. Yü Tsou Ho-shan shu [與鄒鶴山書], HHYC, p. 83.6-13.

_____. "Yüan-ching" [原靜], HHYC, pp. 41.3-42. 3.

_____. "Yüan-hsüeh yüan-chiang" [原學原講], HHYC, pp. 1.1-25.9.

_____. "Yüan-jen" [原人], HHYC, p. 28.2-12.

Keng Ting-hsiang [耿定向]. Kuan-sheng chi [觀生紀], HHYC, p. 140.5-140.11.

Keng Ting-li [耿定力]. Hu Shih-chung i-t'ien chi 胡時中義田記 HHYC, pp. 141.14-143.7.

Li Chih [李贄]. Ho Hsin-yin lun [何心隱論], HHYC, Intro. pp. 10-12.

Tsou Yüan-piao [鄒元標]. Liang Fu-shan chuan [梁夫山傳], HHYC, pp. 120.4-121.15.

Wang Chih-yüan [王之垣]. Li-shih lu [歷仕錄], HHYC, pp. 145.1-146.6.

Wang Shih-chen [王世貞]. Chia-lung Chiang-hu ta-hsia [嘉隆江湖大俠], HHYC, pp. 143.8-144.5.

II. Other Chinese and Japanese Sources

Chi-an fu-chih [吉安府志]. Kuang-hsü ed., 1875.

Chi Wen-fu [嵇文甫]. "Li Cho-wu yü tso-p'ai Wang-hsüeh [李卓吾與左派王學], Ho-nan ta-hsüeh hsüeh-pao [河南大學學報], I-II (1934), 1-8.

160

_____. Tso-p'ai Wang-hsüeh [左派王學]. Shang-hai: K'ai-ming shu-tien, 1934.

_____. Wan-Ming ssŭ-hsiang shih [晚明思想史]. Chungking: Shang-wu yin-shu kuan, 1944.

Chia K'ai [甲凱]. Sung-Ming hsin-hsüeh p'ing-shu [宋明心學評述]. Taipei: Shang-wu yin-shu kuan, 1967.

Ch'ien Mu [錢穆]. Kuo-shih ta-kang [國史大綱]. 2 vols. Chungking: Shang-wu yin-shu kuan, 1940.

_____. Sung-Ming li-hsüeh kai-shu [宋明理學概述]. 3rd ed. 2 vols. Taipei: Chung-hua wen-hua ch'u-pan shih-yeh she, 1962.

Chou I [周易]. Vol. I in Shih-san-ching chu-shu [十三經注疏]. 3d ed. 8 vols. Taipei: I-wen yin-shu kuan, 1965.

Chou Tun-yi [周敦頤]. T'ung-shu [通書]. Ssŭ-pu pei-yao ed. Taipei: Chung-hua shu-chü, 1966.

Fung Yu-lan [馮友蘭]. Chung-kuo che-hsüeh shih pu [中國哲學史補]. 2d ed. Shanghai: Shang-wu yin-shu kuan, 1938.

Ho Tzu-p'ei [何子培]. "Ming-ju Liang Fu-shan hsien-sheng nien-p'u" [明儒梁夫山先生年譜], Chung-fa ta-hsüeh yüeh-k'an [中法大學月刊], V, 5 (1934), 82-95.

Hou Wai-lu [侯外廬]. Chung-kuo ssŭ-hsiang

t'ung-shih [中國思想通史]. 2d ed. 5 vols., IV in 2 pts. Peking: Jen-min ch'u-pan she, 1963.

_____. "Shih-liu shih-chi Chung-kuo te chin-pu te che-hsüeh ssü-ch'ao kai-shu" [十六世紀中國的進步的哲學思潮概述], Li-shih yen-chiu [歷史研究], X (1959), 39-59.

Hsieh Wen-chiung [解文炯]. Liang Fu-shan hsien-sheng i-chi hsü [梁夫山先生遺集序], HHYC, pp. 129.7-131.9.

Hu Shih [胡適]. Lun hsüeh chin chu [論學近著]. 2 vols. Shanghai: K'ai-ming shu-tien, 1935.

Huai Hsin [懷辛]. "Kuan-yü Ho Hsin-yin te chu-tso" [關於何心隱的著作], Li-shih yen-chiu [歷史研究], IX (1958), n.p.

Huang Tsung-hsi [黃宗羲]. Ming-ju hsüeh-an [明儒學案]. 12 vols. Shanghai: Shang-wu yin-shu kuan, 1930.

Jung Chao-tsu [容肇祖]. Ho Hsin-yin chi [何心隱集]. Peking: Chung-hua shu-chü, 1960.

_____. "Ho Hsin-yin chi ch'i ssu-hsiang" [何心隱及其思想], Fu-jen hsüeh-chih [輔仁學誌], VI, 1-2 (1931), 129-170.

_____. "Ho Hsin-yin yüan-szu-shih k'ao" [何心隱寃死事考], Ta kung-pao [大公報], IC (Tientsin, 1936), 4.

_____. Ming-tai ssu-hsiang shih [明代思想史].
   Shanghai: K'ai-ming shu-tien, 1941.

[Kiangsi] sheng-chih pen-chuan [江西省志本傳],
   HHYC, pp. 124.13-125.4.

Ku Ying-t'ai [谷應泰]. Ming-shih chi-shih pen-mo
   [明史紀事本末]. 2 vols., consecutive
   pagination. Taipei: San-min shu-chü, 1963.

Kusumoto, Masatsugu [楠本正継]. Sō-Min jidai
   jugaku shisō no kenkyū [宋明時代儒學思
   想の研究]. 2d ed. Tokyo: Kochi gakuen
   shuppambu, 1964.

Li Chi [禮記]. Vol. V in Shih-san-ching chu-shu
   [十三經注疏]. 3d ed. 8 vols. Taipei:
   I-wen yin-shu kuan, 1965.

Li Chieh [黎傑]. Ming-shih [明史]. 2d ed.
   Taipei: Ta-hsin shu-chü, 1965.

Liang Wei-han [梁維翰]. Liang Fu-shan i-chi pa
   [梁夫山遺集跋], HHYC, p. 132.7-14.

Lun Yü [論語]. Vol. VIII in Shih-san-ching chu-
   shu [十三經注疏]. 3d ed. 8 vols.
   Taipei: I-wen yin-shu, 1965.

Lung Wen-pin [龍文彬]. Ming hui-yao [明會要].
   2 vols., consecutive pagination. Peking:
   Chung-hua shu-chü, 1956.

Matsuzaki, Tsuruo [松崎鶴雄] "Jūroku-shichi
   seiki Chūgoku shisō no kenkyū" [十六七世紀中
   國思想の研究], Mammō [滿蒙], XVII, 1-5

(1936), 86-96, 350-359, 516-523, 711-716, 920-925.

Meng Tzu [孟子]. Vol. VIII in Shih-san-ching chu-shu [十三經注疏]. 3d ed. 8 vols. Taipei: I-wen yin-shu, 1965.

Ming-jen chuan-chi tzu-liao so-yin [明人傳記 資料索引]. 2 vols., consecutive pagination. Taipei: Kuo-li chung-yang t'u-shu-kuan, 1965.

Ming-shih [明史]. 6 vols., consecutive pagination. Taipei: Kuo-fang yen-chiu yüan, 1962.

Ming-shih-kao [明史稿]. 7 vols. Taipei: Wen-hai ch'u-pan she, 1962.

Ming ti-li chih-t'u [明地理志圖]. Hsüan-t'ung ed., 1909.

Okada, Takehiko [岡田武彥]. "Ō-mon genjōha no keitō [王門現成派の系統], Teoria [テオリア], VIII (1965), 31-50.

Okada, Takehiko. Ō Yō-mei to Minmatsu no Jugaku [王陽明と明末の儒學], Tokyo: Myotoku Shuppan-sha, 1970.

Ōkubo, Hideko [大久保英子]. "Taishū gakkō no shominsei" [泰州學校の庶民性], Tōhō shūkyō [東方宗教], III (1953), 49, 90.

Ono, Kazuko [小野和子]. "Jukyo no itansha tachi" [儒教の異端者たち], Taido suru Ajia [胎動するアジア]. Edited by Matsumoto

164

Sannosuke [松本三之介]. Tokyo: Heibon-
sha, 1966, pp. 1-24.

Shang Shu [尚書]. Vol. I in Shih-san ching chu-
shu [十三經注疏]. 3d ed. 8 vols. Taipei:
I-wen yin-shu kuan, 1965.

Shen Te-fu [沈德符]. Yeh-huo-pien [野獲編].
Tao-kuang ed., 1827.

Shimada, Kenji [島田虔次]. "Chūgoku kinsei
no shukan yuishinron ni tsuite" [中國近世の
主觀唯心論について], Tōhōgakuhō [東方學
報], XXVIII (1958), 1-80.

_____. Chūgoku ni okeru kindai shii no zasetsu
[中國に於る近代思惟の挫折]. Tokyo:
Chikuma shobō, 1949.

_____. "Ō-gaku saha ron hihan no hihan" [王学左
派論批判の批判], Shigaku zasshi [史學
雜誌], LXI, 9 (1952), 70-94.

Sung-shih [宋史]. Vols. VI-VII in Erh-shih-wu
shih [二十五史]. 9 vols., consecutive
pagination. Hong Kong: Wen-hsüeh yen-chiu
she, 1959.

Sung ti-li chih-t'u [宋地理志圖]. Hsüan-t'ung
ed., 1904.

T'an Ch'ien [談遷]. Kuo-ch'üeh [國榷]. Peking:
Ku-chi ch'u-pan she, 1958.

Wu K'ang [吳康]. Sung-Ming li-hsüeh [宋明理
學]. 2d rev. ed. Taipei: Hua-kuo ch'u-

pan she, 1962.

Yamamoto, Shōichi [山本正一]. "Ō-gaku no matsu-
ryū ni tsuite"[王學の末流について], <u>Tōhō</u>
<u>bunka</u> <u>gakuhō</u> [東方文化学報], IV (1941),
43-70.

Yamashita, Ryūji [山下龍一]. "[Mindai] gaku-
mon no fukkō to sono fukyū" [明代学問の復
興とその普及], <u>Sekaishi</u> <u>Taikei</u> [世界史
大系], VIII (1957), 216-228.

_____. "Minmatsu ni okeru han jukyō shisō no gen-
ryū" [明末に於る反儒教思想の願,
<u>Tetsugaku</u> <u>zasshi</u> [哲学雑誌], (June, 1951),
66-81.

<u>Yüan</u> <u>ti-li</u> <u>chih-t'u</u> [元地理志圖]. Hsüan-t'ung
ed., 1909.

[<u>Yung-feng</u>] <u>hsien-chih</u> <u>pen-chuan</u> [永豐縣志,
本傳], <u>HHYC</u>, pp. 125.5-126.6.

III. Western Language Sources

Bruce, J. P., <u>Chu</u> <u>Hsi</u> <u>and</u> <u>His</u> <u>Masters</u>. London:
Probsthain, 1923.

Chan, Wing-tsit. <u>A</u> <u>Source</u> <u>Book</u> <u>in</u> <u>Chinese</u> <u>Philos-</u>
<u>ophy</u>. Princeton: Princeton University Press,
1965.

_____ (trans.). <u>Instructions</u> <u>for</u> <u>Practical</u> <u>Living</u>.
New York and London: Columbia University
Press, 1963.

166

_____ (trans.). Reflections on Things at Hand.
New York and London: Columbia University
Press, 1967.

_____. "The Evolution of the Confucian Concept of
Jen," Philosophy East and West, IV, 4 (January,
1955), 295-319.

Chêng, Tê-k'un. Archeology in Ancient China. 2
vols. Cambridge: Heffer, 1959-1960.

Crawford, Robert. The Life and Thought of Chang
Chü-cheng, 1525-1582. Unpublished Ph.D.
dissertation, University of Washington, 1961.

Creel, Herrlee Glessner. Confucius and the Chinese
Way. New York: Harper Torchbooks, 1960.

de Bary, William Theodore. "A Reappraisal of Neo-
Confucianism," Studies in Chinese Thought.
Edited by Arthur F. Wright. Chicago: Univer-
sity of Chicago Press, 1953, pp. 81-111.

_____. "Individualism and Humanitarianism in Late
Ming Thought," Self and Society in Ming Thought.
Edited by William Theodore de Bary. New
York and London: Columbia University Press,
1970, pp. 145-247.

_____. "Some Common Tendencies in Neo-Confucianism,"
Confucianism in Action. Edited by David S.
Nivison and Arthur F. Wright. Stanford:
Stanford University Press, 1959, pp. 25-49.

_____(ed.). The Buddhist Tradition in China, India, and Japan. New York: Modern Library, 1969.

_____, Wing-tsit Chan, and Burton Watson (comps.). Sources of Chinese Tradition. New York and London: Columbia University Press, 1960.

Fairbank, John K., and Edwin O. Reischauer. East Asia: The Great Tradition. Boston: Houghton Mifflin, 1960.

Fingarette, Herbert. Confucius: The Secular as Sacred. New York: Harper and Row, 1972.

Franke, Wolfgang. An Introduction to the Sources of Ming History. Kuala Lumpur: University of Malaya Press, 1968.

Fung, Yu-lan. History of Chinese Philosophy. Translated by Derk Bodde. 2d ed. 2 vols. Princeton: Princeton University Press, 1952, 1953.

Graham, A. C. (trans.). The Book of Lieh-tzu. London: John Murray, 1961.

_____. "The Dialogue Between Yang Ju [楊朱] and Chyntzyy [禽子]," Bulletin of the School of Oriental and African Studies, XXII, 2 (June, 1959), 291-299.

Graham, A. C. Two Chinese Philosophers. Ch'eng Ming-tao and Ch'eng Yi-ch'uan. London: Lund Humphries, 1958.

Ho, Ping-ti. "Early Ripening Rice in Chinese History," Economic History Review, 2d ser., IX,

2 (December, 1956), 200-218.

_____. The Ladder of Success in Imperial China: Aspects of Social Mobility, 1368-1911. New York and London: Columbia University Press, 1962.

Hucker, Charles O. "An Index of Terms and Titles in 'Government Organization of the Ming Dynasty,'" Harvard Journal of Asian Studies, XXIII (1960-1961), 127-151.

_____. "Governmental Organization of the Ming Dynasty," Harvard Journal of Asian Studies, XXI (December, 1958), 1-66.

_____. The Censorial System of Ming China. Stanford: Stanford University Press, 1966.

_____. The Traditional State in Ming Times. Tucson: University of Arizona Press, 1961.

Hwa Yol Jung. "Jen: An Existential and Phenomenological Problem of Intersubjectivity," Philosophy East and West, XVI, 3-4 (July-October, 1966), 169-187.

_____. "Wang Yang-Ming and Existential Phenomenology," International Philosophical Quarterly, V (December, 1965), 613-636.

Ku, Chieh-kang. "A Study of Literary Persecution During the Ming," translated by L. C. Goodrich, Harvard Journal of Asian Studies, III (1938), 254-311.

Legge, James (trans.), Confucian Analects. Vol. I
in The Chinese Classics. 2d rev. ed. 7 vols.
Oxford: Clarendon Press, 1895.

_____ (trans.). The Doctrine of the Mean. Vol. I
in The Chinese Classics. 2d rev. ed. 7 vols.
Oxford: Clarendon Press, 1895.

_____ (trans.). The Great Learning. Vol. I in The
Chinese Classics. 2d rev. ed. 7 vols. Oxford:
Clarendon Press, 1895.

_____ (trans.). The She King or The Book of Poetry.
Vol. IV in The Chinese Classics. 2d rev. ed.
7 vols. Oxford: Clarendon Press, 1895.

_____ (trans.). The Shoo King or The Book of His-
torical Documents. Vol. III in The Chinese
Classics. 2d rev. ed. 7 vols. Oxford:
Clarendon Press, 1895.

_____ (trans.). The Texts of Taoism. 2 vols.
New York: Dover Press, 1962.

_____ (trans.). The Works of Mencius. Vol. II
in The Chinese Classics. 2d rev. ed. 7
vols. Oxford: Clarendon Press, 1895.

_____ (trans.). I Ching: Book of Changes. Edited
by Ch'u Chai and Winberg Chai. New Hyde Park:
University Books, 1964.

Liang, Ch'i-ch'ao. Intellectual Trends in the
Ch'ing Period. Translated by Immanuel C. Y.
Hsü. Cambridge: Harvard University Press,

1959.

Liu, James T. C. <u>Ou-yang</u> <u>Hsiu</u>, <u>An Eleventh Century</u>
<u>Neo-Confucianist</u>. Stanford: Stanford Univer-
sity Press, 1967.

Liu, Wu-chi. <u>A Short History of Confucian Philos-</u>
<u>ophy</u>. n.p., n.d.

Meskill, John. "Academies and Politics in the Ming
Dynasty," <u>Chinese Government in Ming Times</u>.
Edited by Charles O. Hucker. New York and
London: Columbia University Press, 1969, pp.
149-174.

Mote, Frederick W. "Confucian Eremitism in the Yüan
Period," <u>The Confucian Persuasion</u>. Edited by
Arthur F. Wright. Stanford: Stanford Univer-
sity Press, 1960, pp. 202-240.

Okada, Takehiko. "The Chu Hsi and Wang Yang-ming
Schools at the end of the Ming and Tokugawa
Periods," <u>Philosophy East and West</u>, XXIII,
1-2 (January and April, 1973), 139-162.

Takakusu, Junjiro. <u>Essentials of Buddhist Philos-</u>
<u>ophy</u>. 3d ed. Honolulu: University of Hawaii
Press, 1956.

T'an, Po-fu, and Kung-wen Wen (trans.). <u>Economic</u>
<u>Dialogues in Ancient China: Selections from</u>
<u>the Kuan-tzu</u>. Carbondale: Southern Illinois
University Press, 1954.

Wang, Tch'ang-tche. _La Philosophie Morale de Wang Yang-ming_. Paris: P. Geunther, 1936.

Wilhelm, Richard (trans.). _The I Ching or Book of Changes_. Translated from German by Cary F. Baynes. 2d ed. New York: Bollingen Foundation, 1966.

GLOSSARY

This glossary includes names and terms of central
importance in the foregoing discussion of Confucianism, Neo-Confucianism and the life and thought
of Ho Hsin-yin. Names of peripheral importance
are excluded.

a 何心隱

b 泰州學派

c 仁

d 君子

e 張載

f 氣

g 程顥

h 朱熹

i 程頤

j 明太祖

k 明成祖

l 四書大全

m 五經大全

n 性理大全

o 王陽明

p 良知

q 致良知

r 格物

s 意

t 事

u 王艮

v 管子

w 管仲

x 葉伯巨

y	王守仁,伯安,陽明	ap	張居正
z	王艮,汝止,心齋	aq	嚴嵩
aa	梁汝元	ar	原學原講
ab	永豐,吉安,江西	as	柱乾,夫山
ac	顏鈞	at	山農
ad	徐樾	au	子直,波石
ae	趙貞吉	av	孟靜,大洲
af	游俠	aw	近約,二蒲
ag	阮中和	ax	惟德,近溪
ah	聚和堂	ay	懷蘇
ai	程學顏	az	在倫,天臺
aj	程學博	ba	子庸,楚侹
ak	羅汝芳	bb	叔大,太岳
al	錢同文	bc	事
am	耿定向	bd	性
an	耿定理	be	周敦頤
ao	會館	bf	命

bg	中心	bx	陰陽
bh	道心	by	朋友
bi	陽	bz	五事
bj	意氣	ca	貌
bk	義	cb	言
bl	家	cc	視
bm	身	cd	聽
bn	理	ce	思
bo	事	cf	事
bp	物	cg	無欲
bq	友	ch	乘
br	講	ci	治
bs	君	cj	治める
bt	王元	ck	因
bu	元	cl	御
bv	儒	cm	貿
bw	友朋	cn	人心

co 格

cp 格物

cq 圜

cr 圜教

cs 儒

ct 皇

cu 王

cv 張儀

cw 蘇秦

cx 天理

cy 理